FIRE AND SPICE

FIRE  AND SPICE

The Cuisine of Sri Lanka

by
**Heather Jansz Balasuriya
and Karin Winegar**

Illustrated by Susan Friesen

McGRAW-HILL PUBLISHING COMPANY
New York   St. Louis   San Francisco   Auckland   Bogotá   Hamburg
London   Madrid   Mexico   Milan   Montreal   New Delhi   Paris
São Paulo   Singapore   Sydney   Tokyo   Toronto

1 2 3 4 5 6 7 8 9 DOC DOC 8 9 2 1 0 9

ISBN 0-07-003549-0

Library of Congress Cataloging-in-Publication Data

Balasuriya, Heather Jansz.
  Fire and spice.
  Bibliography: p.
  Includes index.
  1. Cookery, Sri Lankan. I. Winegar, Karin.
  II. Title.
  TX724.5.S72B35   1989   641.59549'3   88-26791
  ISBN 0-07-003549-0

Book design by Eve Kirch

Contents

Illustrations

Frontispiece and page 150: This doorway is virtually all that remains of Negombo Fort, 30 miles south of Colombo, built by the Portuguese in the seventeenth century to protect their spice trading dock.

Chapter openers: The Lion of Sri Lanka, or *singha*, the national symbol of the island kingdom.

Pages xii, 182: A Kandyan dancer in ceremonial breastplate and head-dress performs during a festival in Kandy, the ancient hill capital of Sri Lanka. His dance movements date back more than 700 years.

Pages 13, 14, 70, 104, 177: Devil dancers wearing demon masks perform rituals to exorcise demons that cause sickness or to call down divine blessings.

Pages 4, 5, 30, 82, 155, 164, 210: Six of twenty-two maidens, all that remain of the 500 nymphs or court ladies portrayed in the rock-cave frescoes of the fortress of Sigiriya, a fifth-century A.D. seat of royalty.

Pages 19, 121: Detail from a masonry temple in Anuradhapura, the capital of Sri Lanka for 1,400 years, until the tenth century.

Page 142: Cluster of blossoms from the Hakgala Botanical Gardens at the foot of Hakgala Peak in the cool upland hills of Sri Lanka.

Pages 52, 172: Lankatilaka Vihara Buddhist shrine in Kandy, completed in 1344 and called "the beauty spot on Lanka's brow."

Pages 63, 98: The Temple of the Tooth, or Dalada Maligawa, in Kandy—the heart of traditional Sri Lankan culture. Legend says that the tooth was saved from Buddha's cremation pyre and smuggled into Sri Lanka in the fourth century A.D. It arrived in Kandy in 1590 and is stored in the inmost of seven gold caskets.

Pages 38, 56, 197: A Kandyan chief in ceremonial costume for the annual Perahera, a procession of lighted and decorated elephants, the largest of which carries the reliquary containing Buddha's tooth. The Perahera is held each August in Kandy.

Pages 8, 206: Drummer accompanying a Kandyan dance. Drum rhythms may imitate the gait of a horse, elephant, or hawk.

Pages 2, 33, 134: A stone lion guards the staircase of Yapahuwa, a 300-foot-high rock fortress surrounded by ramparts and moats. Yapahuwa was the capital of Sri Lanka in the year 1301.

Pages 87, 208: Strolling with a parasol on one of Sri Lanka's sun-swept beaches. Both the West Coast and the less developed East Coast offer hundreds of beaches with opposing monsoon seasons: the West Coast is best from November to April, the East Coast, from May to October.

Pages 108, 204: An elephant in parade costume for the Perahera in Kandy. Elephants have played a part throughout Sri Lanka's history, taking on a variety of roles in agriculture, war, religious processions, and even executions. In the national parks, particularly Ruhuna and Wilpattu, it is still possible to see wild elephants.

Pages 20, 192: Elephant bas-relief at Isurunumiya, Anuradhapura.

Pages x, 202: Tamil tea plucker.

Acknowledgments

With special thanks to Erma Iris Jansz, Marie Pietersz, Terryll Perera, Dawn Bartholomusz, Isabel Loos, Lynn Ramalingam, Aruni Fernando, Chulanganee Fernando, and Mangalika Fernando for their generous advice on family recipes and Sri Lankan customs, to Evan Balasuriya, co-owner of the Sri Lanka Curry House, to computer wizards Bruce Adomeit, Brian A. Cravens, and Al Sicherman for handling all the inscrutable technical details, to Jarrett Smith for last-minute artistic assistance, to food writers and cookbook authors Mary Hart and Ann Burckhardt for advice and the loan of reference material, to Susan Friesen for providing the visual music to our words, to Jack Reuler and Peter Moore for fetching and carrying and especially for emotional sustenance, to the Book Group, whose every meal is a feast and who introduced us to Susan, to photographers Doug Beasley and Judy Olausen for making us look almost as delicious as the food looks, and to Wally and Deanne Winegar, two of Minnesota's greatest cooks.

—**Karen Winegar**

Introduction

There is no hotter cuisine, no food more fiery, aromatic, and vivid than the cooking of Sri Lanka—not Mexican, with its deep tones of cumin, and not Thai, with its tart-hot team of lemongrass and limes. Sri Lankan food leaves even the monotone chili-oil hotness of Szechuan back in the tamer territory of the tongue.

As we Americans discovered the pleasures and excitement of spicy cuisine over the past decade or two, we have become more adventurous about exploring hot cuisine for ourselves. We are gradually making a pilgrimage of the palate, moving from Cantonese to Szechuan cooking, from Peking-style to Vietnamese cuisine, from American to Tex-Mex, Cajun, and Mexican dishes, and on from all these to the more exotic fringes of cuisine such as Thai, Cambodian, Indian, and Afghani.

There is one restaurant in the United States that serves the cooking of Sri Lanka—the Sri Lanka Curry House in Minneapolis, Minnesota. Because it is the only restaurant specializing in Sri Lankan cuisine, those who would like to try Ceylon-style food may have to create it for themselves. For this truly exciting culinary adventure, *Fire and Spice* is the perfect native guide.

CHAPTER 1

THE RESPLENDENT LAND*

The island of Sri Lanka—known as Ceylon before its independence from Great Britain in 1948—lies in the Indian Ocean, 30 miles south of the tip of India. *Sri Lanka* means "resplendent land" in Sinhalese, and it is an old, old land, with more than 2,500 years of recorded history.

At one time, the island was called Tambapanni. Greek sailors changed that name to Taprobane. And Arab explorers called it Serendib—the origin of the word *serendipity*, "to make a happy chance discovery."

For centuries, Sri Lanka has been a source of gems, especially sapphires and moonstones, as well as copra (made from the dried kernel of the coconut), coffee, cocoa, rubber, and cinnamon. Ceylon tea is considered the best in the world. And the country has some of the best beaches in the world, too: My favorites are the coral gardens where the beach looks like a large swimming pool.

*This introductory chapter was written by Heather Jansz Balasuriya.

At beach level, you'll find sand, surf, and coconut palms, and the average year-round temperature is 90°F. But nearby in the hills at 6,000 feet, the climate is cool and sometimes wet. (Some areas of the island get more than 100 inches of rain a year.) The English and Scottish planters who established tea plantations here in the 1700s found this up-country climate particularly delightful and comfortable.

The island, nicknamed "The Pearl of the Indian Ocean" for its teardrop shape and richness, is home to 15 million people, chiefly of three ethnic groups: the majority—about 70 percent —are Sinhalese (*singha* means "lion"), who are mostly Buddhists. Theirs is the official language of Sri Lanka. The Tamils, who are Hindus, make up about 15 to 20 percent of the population; they often speak only Tamil and English. The Sinhalese are descended from Aryan tribes, and the Tamils from Dravidians. The smallest group are Dutch Burghers, which is my heritage; they are of mixed Portuguese and Dutch ancestry.

Our flag depicts this potpourri of races. The lion on the Sri

Lankan flag is linked to a legendary princess who mated with a lion and became mother of the Sinhalese people. The green stripe on the flag symbolizes the Tamil people. The orange is for the Muslims. The four leaves represent the bo tree under which Buddha attained enlightenment, and the maroon color represents the kings of the island.

Throughout the country, men wear a sarong and women wear a *saree*, a long piece of cloth wrapped gracefully around the body and fastened at the waist, and a blouse with short puffy sleeves (called a *choli*, or jacket).

Babies are adorned with black wrist and ankle bangles to keep away the evil eye. A dot of saffron, called a *potu*, is placed on the child's forehead in the location of the "third eye" (pineal gland). The potu is said to prevent the baby from being hypnotized by the evil eye. Sri Lankans consider it bad luck to say good things about a baby, since compliments might attract the attention of the evil eye.

The dots on the forehead are worn by adults, too. Traditionally, unmarried women wear a black dot, married women wear red or other colors. But some Sinhalese girls simply coordinate the dots with their clothes until they are married.

Color is important in Sri Lankan dress: black is considered unattractive—if not inauspicious. Many women won't wear dark colors at all because of the general belief that dark colors are associated with unhappiness. At temple ceremonies and in funerals, the appropriate color to wear is white.

Then there is the bright saffron of the monks' robes. Nearly three-quarters of Sri Lankans are Buddhists, and there are three main sects, or *nikayas*, of Buddhism represented in the country: Ramayana, Amarapura, and Siyam.

Traditionally, monks had to beg for their food from house to house each morning because religious custom forbids them from eating after noon, and some monks still continue the begging. But now, most communities around a temple are organized so that different families provide the meals each day for the monks.

Giving alms to monks is still customary, and they are also invited into Sri Lankan homes to celebrate weddings, funerals, or anniversaries where they share very elaborately cooked meals. There can be as many as seventy to one-hundred people at these festive parties where sumptuous amounts of rice and curry are served, generally including several fish curries (monks do not eat meat). The meal concludes with sweetmeats (cookies or toffee), pudding, ice cream or curd, and fruit.

In many ways, the past is very much alive in Sri Lanka. Arranged marriages are still common, although they have been modified over the centuries—today, *arranged* does not mean "forced." A wedding is performed only if both people give their consent.

Before the two individuals meet, their parents may have an astrologer compare the young peoples' horoscopes to see if they are a good match. Even if the match looks promising, the couple must wait for the "auspicious" time to marry, and they must be of compatible astrological signs. At one time it was a tradition for girls to marry much-older men, and although this practice is less common now, it's still considered desirable that the man be at least one year older than the woman.

The ideal of female beauty hasn't really changed in Sri Lanka in a thousand years or more: The long hair, alluring eyes, and full breasts of the maidens depicted in the 800-year-old frescoes at the old fortress of Sigiriya are still considered the epitome of grace and beauty.

In many other ways, the previous centuries live on in Sri Lanka. The caste system still exists in some form: The two basic divisions are called *giogama*, or farmers, and *karava*, or fishermen, who were once associated with the warrior class.

For young people, the current ideal is to get a job in engineering or medicine; higher education is very important to Sri Lankans, especially among the middle and upper classes.

Tea and coffee plantations were first introduced by the British in the eighteenth century, and tea is still a major industry. Tea pickers pick by hand and throw the leaves over their shoulder into a basket hanging on their backs. Tea is picked every ten days or so to get the tender new leaves from the top of all the tea plants.

Sri Lankans celebrate many religious festivals throughout the year, and each is an occasion for ceremonial feasts and treats. Every August there is the Kandy Perahera (*perahera* means "procession") in the city of Kandy in which elephants in lavishly bejeweled costumes and trailing strings of electric lights parade in honor of a holy relic, said to be the Buddha's tooth.

A princess was thought to have smuggled the tooth—salvaged from Buddha's funeral pyre—into Sri Lanka in her hair in the fourth century A.D. The tooth is kept in seven gold caskets in a moated temple called the Dalada Maligawa in the city of Kandy. When it is carried by the *tusker*, or largest elephant, white sheets are rolled out especially for him.

Another exotic festival, the Vel, takes place in June. It includes a parade in which people carry the statue of a saint from one temple in a suburb of Colombo to another.

Wesak comes during the full moon in May and is the celebration of the birth and death of the Buddha—it's like Christmas and Easter combined. Hindus celebrate Thai Pongal, a sort of Thanksgiving day in January. For forty days each year, Moslems hold Ramadan—the ninth month of the Islamic year, observed as sacred with fasting from sunrise to sunset. And one festival that Tamils and Sinhalese celebrate together is the New Year celebration in April; during this festival, everyone visits neighbors and relatives and consults astrologers.

Sri Lankans are warm people—sociable, talkative, and generous. Punctuality is not considered a priority. Invited for dinner at six, they are likely to arrive at eight and sit for a couple of hours to talk before eating. Life is lived at a leisurely pace.

Sri Lankans are especially hospitable and enjoy welcoming visitors into their homes to share a rice-and-curry meal—including American tourists who have come the approximately 9,000 miles from the United States to their exotic island.

CHAPTER 2

COOKING IN SRI LANKA

The cuisine of Sri Lanka reflects the influence of centuries of trade with India, Arabia, Malaysia, Portugal, the Netherlands, and Great Britain.

As traders and conquerors invaded the island, they left their marks on its cuisine, the most recent influence being British, who arrived in 1815. As a result, recipes today include items from half a dozen cultures.

Although many Sri Lankans are descended from Indians who migrated to this beautiful island centuries ago, their cuisine has evolved with some distinct differences: Sri Lankan cuisine is much hotter in general than Indian cuisine, and while Indians use ingredients such as tamarind, mint, yogurt, and cucumber extensively in their curries, Sri Lankans use more seeni sambol and goraka (see the glossary for explanations of these terms). Where Indians use water, Sri Lankan use coconut milk. And Sri Lankan vegetable dishes are not cooked as long as their softer, creamier Indian counterparts.

The British influence can still be seen in ingredients the Sri

Lankans have adapted such as treacle, marmite, and vegemite. (Coconut treacle is a molasseslike sweet syrup made from the coconut flower.) Sri Lankans eat "curd and honey" for dessert, which is really yogurt with coconut treacle drizzled over the top.

Vegemite and Marmite are pastelike, bottled yeast extracts (vegemite is meatless) that add a British flavor. While the British and Australians use them as a breakfast spread on buttered toast, Sri Lankans melt a tablespoon or two in water as a drink for children or use them as a sort of broth.

Traces of British culture abound in food terminology. For example, Sri Lankans speak of *rashers*, or "strips," of bacon; *castor*, or "granulated," sugar; and a gill of something (a *gill* is about ¼ pint). What the West calls "powdered sugar," Sri Lankans refer to as *icing sugar*, and they don't "frost a cake," they *ice* it. Large green sweet peppers are called *capsicum* rather than "bell peppers." "Napkins" are *serviettes*, and "vanilla extract" is called *essence*.

The dominant cookbook in Sri Lanka for many years was the British mainstay, *Mrs. Beaton's*. And the very few cookbooks published in Sri Lanka today contain British recipes for everything from jellied calves' foot to jugged hare—hardly dishes deeply rooted in ancient island custom.

But the central foods of Sri Lanka remain the indigenous ones, with *bath* ("rice") being the most important. In fact, Sri Lankans don't ask, "Have you eaten?" They ask, "Have you eaten rice?" ("*Bath kavatha?*")

Rice and curry with thousands of variations of ingredients, seasoning, and accompaniment are the staple foods, typical for lunch and dinner. And depending on the seasoning, the curries are white, brown, black, or red. In my family, leftover rice was tempered with onions and hot peppers, or red chilies and mustard seed, and we had it for breakfast with a hot *sambol*, a condiment used to spice up a meal. The hot sambol can also be served as a side dish. Even if the rice and curry are bland and unremarkable, the sambol—and there are hundreds of different kinds of sambols—always makes it a meal.

Unlike Western cooking, Sri Lankan meals are not divided into appetizers and entrées designed to be eaten as separate courses. One might encounter such a division in restaurants, perhaps, but not in homes. In the home you will be served many dishes all at once. The rice is placed on a large platter with various curries in tiny containers. You will be given a spoon to serve yourself, placing rice in the middle of your plate and surrounding it with the curries. Then you mix a little of everything in nimbly and gracefully with your fingers.

A big dish of plain rice is usually served with one meat, or more often, a fish. At special functions, there is yellow rice cooked in coconut milk with lots of cardamom and turmeric or an elaborate dish called *lampries* (from the Dutch word *lomprijst* but pronounced "lump-rice") made with meatballs and sambols. More than a dozen varieties of rice are grown in Sri Lanka including short and long grains and fat and pearly grains, ranging from the common white to reddish purple.

Each meal has a few curries—most often curried *dhal* (pureed lentils)—and one or two green vegetables, such as a vegetable mallung and a vegetable curry. These dishes are normally cooked with a moderate amount of spice, because not everyone eats them hot. However, there are always the hot sambols, lime pickles, and spicy chutneys.

More fish is consumed than red meat in Sri Lanka, and we eat many kinds of fish, some of which are native to Sri Lanka with no equivalent Western names. Among the favorites are seer fish, thora malu, parah malu, and kingfish.

At home, it is the custom to eat deftly with the fingers of your right hand. If company comes, we set out silverware, but everyone still eats with fingers—foreigners find this messy but fun. Somehow eating with your hands makes you want to eat more. (In restaurants, Sri Lankans do use silverware.)

In Sri Lanka, food is considered a gift from the gods. Harvesting is scheduled to coincide with auspicious times determined by the astrologers; the first portion is given to the gods. When grain is harvested, it's never placed on the ground, out of respect. When you eat a meal in Sri Lanka, it's considered a mark of respect and gratitude to finish all the food on your plate.

They say Sri Lanka is one-hundred years behind the United States in many ways: Television was unavailable until about 1977, and pizza and hamburgers arrived only about 1985 or so, and then only in Colombo, the capital. (The chain restaurants have yet to arrive.) And thirty miles outside the city, you still feel as if you're in the nineteenth century.

This is an advantage, however, when it comes to food, because the produce is fresh and raised naturally, not processed. In many areas, fruit sellers and fishermen still come to the houses on foot, by bicycle, or in a van each morning bringing their fresh wares—mackerel, seer fish, sardines, smelt, ripe mangos, passion fruit, papaya, and pineapple. There are hard-shelled, brown-skinned woodapples; green and yellow guavas; and tart red "lovie" fruit, the size of cherries.

Because labor is very inexpensive, many middle-class people have servants in Sri Lanka: The wealthy families sometimes have one for each chore. Our family sometimes had servants for half the day, so that it was in the making of dinner at night that my sisters and I learned to cook.

No one ever "cooks by the book" in Sri Lanka: The standard Sinhalese method is a pinch of this and a pinch of that. Old cookbooks measure ingredients by the sprig, wineglass, dessert spoon, teacup, pinch, or bundle. Even using the same ingredients, a dish will naturally turn out differently if prepared by two different people.

If somebody asks me, how much of a given ingredient I put in, I show the amount with my hand, say, four fingers and a thumb. It's a visual tradition. When you cook on your own, you will discover it's a trial-and-error method. In cooking portions for restaurant use, I learned to measure the ingredients and have used this clarified system for the book. But it's not a rigid

system, and you should feel free to experiment with the recipes and alter them to suit your own taste.

With refrigeration, prepackaged foods, freezers, tools, and microwaves, cooking in the Western world is relatively easy. But for old-style, authentic Sri Lankan cooking, you really do need at least two people in the kitchen. Washing the rice, picking out the stones, scraping coconut, boiling the meat, and so on is a full day's job. Many people get up at 4 or 5 a.m. to start breakfast and then go right on to prepare lunch.

Early in the morning, the servants start to cook, roasting and grinding the spices and herbs and molding them into spice balls. We use a grinding stone, which is an oblong pillow of stone and a roller. Although primitive, it's used even in the richest of homes. It grinds the spices very fine, and it allows for a great deal of control. One can get just the right "feel" of the grind and adjust this feel to each spice. The ground spices are formed into balls. Sometimes the spices are ground again and made into a paste just before they are used. Whoever cooks meals during the day will just take a pinch from the spice balls for the curries.

In some homes, the "cookwoman," or "cookie," does all the spice grinding. In others, a woman comes in one or twice a week to grind spices.

Generally, the next step is dry roasting. What makes the taste of Sri Lankan food different from Indian curries is that the spices are toasted in a dry skillet until they are dark. This gives food a different flavor and aroma from that of Indian dishes. We also cook only with sea salt, storing the coarse rocklike salt in a bottle of water and sprinkling it through our fingers into the food.

Marketing is done each day at open-air markets. Until about 1970, most Sri Lankans did not own a refrigerator, and some still do not have one.

There are really two types of kitchens in a rather well-to-do Sri Lankan home: one is a pantry used to prepare three-course meals and cakes. It is generally equipped with stainless steel pans and an electric stove. The other is a more primitive place where cooking is often done over kerosene or over three large bricks containing firewood and where the walls can be very sooty. Clay pots are used in this kitchen, and nothing tastes as good as curry cooked in clay on an open fire.

Cooking in clay seems to take longer than cooking over a gas flame with a steel or earthenware pot. But the resultant flavor is richer, deeper. Clay-cooked curries have a distinctively smoky taste, and the curry is somehow thicker.

It's not eye appeal but nose appeal and taste that perhaps set Sri Lankan cooking apart from other cuisines. Any Sri Lankan meal—cooked in clay over a three-brick charcoal fire in Sri Lanka or in top-flight steel dishes over gas—is a potpourri of aroma that refuses to be sorted out: cardamom and ginger; garlic, onion, and rampa; tomato, Maldive fish, coconut, and lemon.

COCONUT CUISINE

Sri Lankan cooking relies heavily on coconut milk, as opposed to coconut water, which is the liquid inside a young coconut. At 12, I was taught to crack the coconut exactly in half using a cleaver. If you want to try it Sri Lankan style, hold a coconut in the palm of one hand, hit it with the blunt side of a cleaver just once in the middle, and then use the sharp side of the knife to pry it apart.

Sri Lankans scoop out the meat and then grind it by hand in a coconut scraper, which resembles an old-fashioned meat grinder. When the coconut meat is finely shredded, it's put in a big bowl with water and squeezed by hand to extract the thick white milk. In Sri Lanka, the extracting is done three times for a first, second, and third milk, the first being the strongest and thickest. Traditionally, the second and third yields are for cooking vegetables or boiling meat. But when you are making curries and you want a good thick gravy (sauce), you use only the first milk. If you can't get coconut milk, You can substitute 2% milk, regular milk, or light cream—whatever makes a nice thick gravy.

Pol
Coconut

Another product of the palm tree is gingelly oil, which the Tamils use instead of coconut butter for cooking. (They also use it as a body cream for themselves and their babies, since it's supposed to give strength.)

The orange, or king, coconut—called *thambilie*—is used for medicinal purposes. On a hot day, if you don't have time to cool off in a shower, drink the water of an orange coconut —it's considered cooling to your system. It's also used for making *arrak*, or palm toddy.

You may find inexpensive, canned, unsweetened coconut milk at Chinese, Thai, or other oriental markets and stores. Don't cook with the sweetened coconut cream you may find in American grocery stores—that's mostly for mixing piña coladas.

Nestlé makes a dried coconut milk powder (see the list of sources which starts on p. 211) that is excellent. Just mix it with warm water; it tastes exactly like coconut that has been squeezed out Sri Lankan style.

Desiccated, shredded coconut is mature coconut meat that has been scraped out of the shell and dried. In the United States, you can buy it sweetened or unsweetened. Do not use the sweet version for sambols and curries.

CHAPTER 4

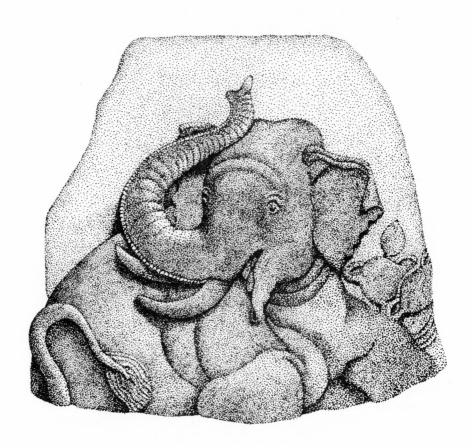

A GLOSSARY OF SRI LANKAN TERMS AND INGREDIENTS

A word about herbs and spices: Most of the spices in the cans and jars on the spice rack of the average Western family home are stale. Exposed to light or heat, spices quickly lose their potency. To get the full effect of a Sri Lankan dish, it's best to use fresh spices. Better still, buy the whole spice and grind it yourself—whole spices keep much longer than ground or powdered spices. Buy small amounts, label them clearly (many of them look alike), and store them in your freezer or any cool, dark place in tightly capped jars or in plastic bags.

Most of the ingredients used in the following recipes can now be found in any city. If for some reason you don't find them or cannot order them from the list of sources which begins on p. 211, use the substitutes suggested below.

Before you set out to prepare a Sri Lankan meal, the following basic shopping list should be assembled (most of it can be obtained at any grocery store; a few items might require a trip to an Asian or Indian grocery): cardamom pods, ground cinnamon and stick cinnamon, ground and whole cloves, ground coriander, ground cumin, curry powder (see Chapter 6, Making Your Own Curry Powder), turmeric, fresh garlic, fresh ginger-root, white or yellow onions, crushed dried red chilies, chili powder, hot green chilies, cider vinegar, vegetable oil, salt, black pepper, lemons, rampa, white or basmati rice, Maldive fish, and dried shrimp.

banana chilies—Firm, long yellow peppers, common in American grocery stores. They are not as hot as their little green cousins, but they can be spicy, especially the small ones. Used in stuffed chilies or deviled shrimp or potato dishes, Sri Lankans call them *malu miris*. (Sometimes also called banana peppers.)

cardamom—Beige papery-textured pods containing small black seeds, very aromatic and said to be good for digestion. Used in Sri Lankan curries, rice dishes, and desserts. They are available in most grocery stores in powder, seed, or whole pod form. Sri Lankans most often use the whole pod, crushing it open with the flat of a knife.

coriander—An herb whose leaves and seeds are commonly used in curries, chutnies, and sambols. It has a fresh, mintlike taste. Sri Lankans use the seed more often than the leaf. In the case of colds, coughs, and fever, Sri Lankans boil two cups of coriander seed with raw ginger and fresh garlic in four or five cups of water and then reduce the liquid to two cups. It becomes a strong black tea, called *kothamalie* in Sinhalese.

curd—The Sri Lankan term for yogurt. Curd is often made with water-buffalo milk.

curry leaves—Edible gray-green leaves that resemble bay leaf, used in flavoring sambols and fish, vegetable, or meat curries. The Sri Lankans use curry leaves fresh, but they can be used dried if fresh leaves are not available. The Sinhalese term for the plant is *karapincha*, and if you can find them fresh, they

Curry leaves Karapincha

add great depth and flavor to a dish. They are not removed before serving, and they are edible. There is no substitute for curry leaves.

cutlets—From the Sinahlese *cutlis*. These patties of seasoned meat or seafood, finely chopped vegetables, and mashed potato are really what Westerners call "croquettes." Sri Lankan cutlets are formed into balls or patties and are usually dipped into beaten egg, and then breaded and fried. They are served either as appetizers or as main courses.

dhal—Cooked, spiced lentils. The combination of rice and dhal is the foundation of any Sri Lankan meal.

dried shrimp—Available in most Asian or Indian grocery stores, these small dried shrimp add intense flavor to Sri Lankan dishes such as sambols or vegetable curries. Salt cod, finely chopped, or Maldive fish may be substituted.

fenugreek—A flowering plant native to western Asia, the leaves of which are dried and ground for curries. Fenugreek has a faintly bitter flavor.

frickadels—Minced meat or fish, shaped in balls, coated with bread crumbs and fried. One of the ingredients in the complicated holiday dish, lampries. (*Frikkadels* is the Dutch word for "force-meat balls," or stuffing made into meatball form.)

ghee—Clarified butter used for frying in Sri Lankan dishes. The advantage of ghee over butter is that is can withstand a higher temperature without burning; so it's good for browning onions and spices. To clarify butter, simply melt two sticks (one-half pound) in a saucepan and simmer it for 20 to 30 minutes very gently until it condenses somewhat. The butter should take on a gold color. Strain it through cheesecloth and store it in a clean, covered jar; it does not need to be refrigerated.

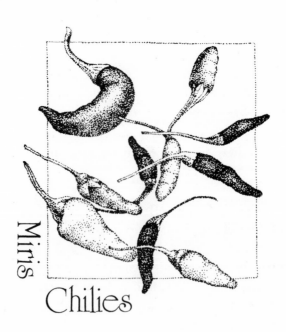

Miris Chilies

gingelly oil—Palm tree oil used in cooking by Tamils instead of coconut butter. They also use it as a body cream for themselves and their babies, since it's supposed to give strength.

goraka—A very tart dried fruit used only in special curry dishes that require a tangy taste, something like a green tomato. It contains acid and has a tendency to tenderize other ingredients. When fresh, it is bright-orange and segmented.

green chilies—The hot ones! Small and fiery. Not to be confused with the big, gently flavored red or green bell peppers that you see in most American supermarkets and gardens. These chilies are essential to Sri Lankan cuisine, and turn up in sambols, in vegetable and meat dishes, as well as in vegetarian dishes. There are many varieties—skinny short ones, skinny long ones. Dried red chilies are just sun-dried green chilies. They are usually available in grocery stores, but jalapeño and serrano chili peppers are acceptable substitutes. Store them in the refrigerator; they do not keep well (they tend to get moldy) or for very long. Another method of preserving them if you do not have regular access to chilies is to wash the fresh chilies, dry them, and store them in a jar of oil, well-capped and in a dark place. You can also pickle them in vinegar and salt if you don't have them often, but in Sri Lanka we get them fresh daily. (Compare: banana chilies). *A cautionary note*: Wash your hands thoroughly after handling chilies, and avoid touching your eyes.

hoppers—A hopper looks something like a crepe before it's folded, something like an English muffin. The word comes from the Tamil *appam* or *apu*, which means clapping with the hands; and that is how hoppers are shaped. They are eaten for breakfast and as snacks along with sambols, with sweetening such as honey or syrup, or with butter and jam. Originally, palm toddy was used for leavening in hoppers, but this has been replaced by yeast.

jackfruit, or **jakfruit**—A cousin of the breadfruit. This enormous green oval fruit with the prickly rind can weigh up to 100 pounds. The juicy yellow flesh can be eaten fresh, avoiding the many seeds, and it is also available canned.

jaggery—A hardened coconut treacle similar to a heavy brown sugar, sometimes melted down and used in desserts or chewed when drinking plain tea. It is made from kitul palm sap. You may substitute refined or raw brown sugar in equal portion with molasses.

lampries—From the Dutch word *lomprijst*. This is an elaborate dish that requires the better part of a day to create. Lampries consists of five ingredients—each a meal in itself—steamed together at the conclusion, although you may serve the frickadels separately. Lampries is a festive holiday or party dish that Sri Lankans serve at Christmas, New Year's, weddings, twenty-first birthdays (the coming of age in Sri Lanka), anniversaries, or other special occasions. Because of the complexity of the dish, there are people who specialize in catering it for parties; it is sometimes also a party dish brought by guests to their host. Although lampries is traditionally made wrapped up in folded and skewered banana or plantain leaves, most cooks who do not have access to banana leaves will be able to substitute a wrapping of aluminum foil.

lemongrass—A flavorful spiky sedge with a bulblike, juicy white base; its long, stiff, slim stalks are green when fresh and turn tan as they dry. It is used in cooking meat or fish curries and seeni sambols. The Sinhalese word for it is *sara*, and it is used fresh, dried, or powdered. Lemon juice makes a fair substitute.

Maldive fish—A dried, salted tuna from the Maldive Islands south of Sri Lanka. Used dried and powdered or chipped, Maldive fish adds flavor and thickness and a slight fishiness to many curries, but not usually the meat or fish varieties. Finely chopped

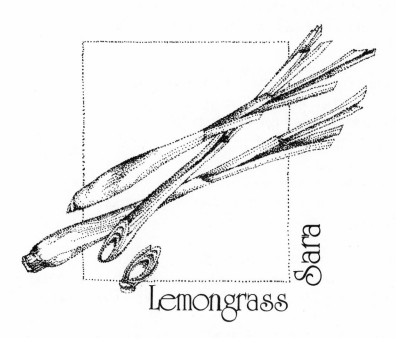

Lemongrass

Sara

salt cod is a fair substitute and so is crushed dried shrimp, both available at any Oriental grocery.

mallung—Sri Lankan term for a vegetable dish cooked with coconut meat. Dried prawn mallung or dried fish mallung are also popular.

Marmite—A concentrated yeast spread from Great Britain made of salt, yeast extract, spices, onions, and carrots. Sri Lankans love it served on buttered toast or as a drink or soup base.

mustard seed—Tan, brown, or black seeds of the mustard plant used in Sri Lankan chutneys and in beef and fish dishes. Usually they are dry-roasted until they pop, to bring out the full flavor, and often they are ground into a paste.

pittu—A steamed flour or rice flour pastry that replaces bread, rice, or rotti in a meal. It is served crumbled or sliced, and is typically eaten for breakfast—although many people like it for dinner.

rampa (pandanus leaf)—Spear-shaped aromatic leaves used to flavor curries. From the lemongrass family, rampa is not edible, but it is used as a flavoring in boiling rice. Sri Lankans do not remove it before serving; they just leave it on the plate.

red chilies—A tree-ripened, hot green chili, crushed and dried, used to flavor dhal, sambols, appetizers, and curries. The Sinhalese word is *valieche miris*.

rottis—(Pronounced row' tees.) A pan-fried soft bread similar to Indian flat breads such as nan and resembling Scandinavian *lefse*. The Sri Lankan versions sometimes contain fresh grated coconut or, if that's not available, desiccated (dry) coconut. Sri Lankans usually serve them with curries and sambols, and they are very popular for breakfast. Rottis can be wrapped around meat or vegetable dishes, or they can be torn with the fingers and dipped into curries and sambols. They may be eaten alone or as a side dish.

rulang—Semolina, a farinalike cereal grain used in cakes and pastries.

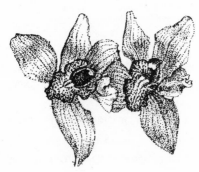

saffron—The rare and expensive pistils of a breed of crocus plant. It lends color, most of all, to rice dishes. (Turmeric is an inexpensive substitute.)

sambol—A condiment or accompaniment to meals. Sambols come in countless varieties: fruit or vegetables and spices—some fiery hot, some not.

seeni sambol—A slow-cooked onion and chili sambol with Maldive fish and a dash of sugar (the Sinhalese word for sugar is *seeni*).

tamarind—A pod-shaped fruit grown on a feathery-looking tree. Tamarind (the word is derived from the Arabic for "Indian date") is used green or ripe (brown) or as a paste. It tenderizes meat and adds zip to sauces and chutneys. Frozen orange juice concentrate can be used as a substitute, or a mixture of six parts vinegar and one part sugar.

treacle—Molasses, traditionally used as a sweetener in British cuisine. Used in Sri Lanka in rice and curry dishes as well as in desserts. Maple syrup makes an acceptable substitute.

turmeric—A powdered, virtually flavorless rhizome used chiefly for the rich yellow color it gives to dishes, especially white curries, rice, and dhal. It is often used as a cheap substitute for saffron. The Sinhalese call it *kaha*.

Vegemite—A salty, dense vegetable paste made in Great Britain, popular among Sri Lankans as a spread.

woodapple—A hard-shelled brownish fruit native to Sri Lanka. In Sri Lanka it is cracked in half and sugar is added and stirred to make a beverage right in the woodapple shell, or it is made into a drink with coconut milk.

CHAPTER 5

SUGGESTED MENUS

Sri Lankans eat less systematically than Americans and Europeans, but if you'd like to use Sri Lankan dishes in a Western style, here are some suggestions for menus based on recipes available in *Fire and Spice*.

If you'd like to serve a more elaborate meal, simply increase the number of sambols and vegetable side dishes, relying on what's in season. The coconut sambol, for example, goes with almost any lunch or dinner menu.

Pastries and desserts are served at tea time rather than after a meal—Sri Lankans tend not to eat baked pastries or ice-cream desserts. Fruit salad or sliced fresh fruit is frequently served following dinner. The variety of fruit available is enormous, from mangosteens, guavas, rambutans, and pomegranates to woodapples. There are about six varieties of plantains (bananas) ranging from finger size to huge yellow ones, both fat and thin.

Here are some brief examples of combinations that Sri Lankans love.

MENU 1

Curried Pork on a Stick
Rice
Curried Dhal (Lentils)
Tempered Chicken Curry
Green Bean Mallung
Coconut Sambol
Fresh Mango Slices

MENU 2

Open-Face Salmon-Stuffed Chilies
Rice
Egg Curry
Broccoli Mallung
Curried Dhal (Lentils)
Cucumber Sambol
Fresh Papaya Halves with Lemon Juice

MENU 3

Beef Cutlets
Plain Rotti
Fish Curry
Fried Onion Sambol
Fruit Salad and Ice Cream

MENU 4

Chutney Chicken Wings
Rice
Lamb Curry
Potato Curry
Coconut Sambol
Kale Mallung
Pineapple Slices with Salt and Pepper

MENU 5

Crab Curry
Yellow or White Rice
Dhal (Lentils)
Hot Green Chili Sambol
Pickled Eggplant
Curd and Honey (Yogurt with Coconut Treacle)

MENU 6

Prawn Curry
White Rice
Green Bean Curry
Cabbage Thaldala
Lunumiris (Onion Chili Sambol)
Avocado Fluff

MENU 7

White Rice
Dhal (Lentils)
Coconut Sambol
Pappadums
Brussels Sprouts Mallung
Milk Toffee (Aluwa)

Curry leaves Karapincha

CHAPTER 6

MAKING YOUR OWN CURRY POWDER

Many Westerners think a curry is any meat dish seasoned with curry powder and served with rice. But in Asia, especially India, Sri Lanka, and Japan, curry is more a *method* of cooking, and it may involve meat, seafood, or vegetables and a wide variety of seasonings. The origins are uncertain, but the word *curry* may derive from the Tamil word for sauce, *kari*.

Real Sri Lankan *curry powder* is a powerfully aromatic blend of dark-roasted spices that may include all or some of the following: cardamom seeds, chilies, cinnamon, cloves, coriander, cumin, fenugreek, tamarind, garlic, ginger, goraka, mustard seed, black pepper, turmeric, lemongrass, and rampa. (See the glossary for explanations of the less common spices.)

Powdered spices may be used if you can't find the whole spices. And the curry powder described below may be substituted in any recipe that calls for cumin or coriander, or both.

If you decide to grind your own spices, a mortar and pestle are superior to using a food processor—the former seems to release the oils and flavors better. But if you don't have one or if time is a factor, the food processor will do.

HEATHER'S ROASTED CURRY POWDER

¼ cup ground cumin
2 tablespoons fennel seeds
3 tablespoons coriander powder
20 to 25 curry leaves
10 cardamom pods, crushed
6 whole cloves
1 tablespoon ground black pepper
6 one-inch pieces rampa
3 one-inch pieces cinnamon stick
1 tablespoon dried, crushed red chilies
1 tablespoon mustard seeds

Start with a large pan, and dry-roast the ingredients separately over low to medium heat, roasting the mustard seeds last. In a few minutes, the mustard seeds will start to pop (keep the lid on the pan or the mustard seeds will fly out). Then stir in the coriander and cumin; when the spices begin to turn light-brown, add the rest of the ingredients. Since the curry powder mix can burn very quickly, stir it continuously. Roast the spices for about 7 to 10 minutes, until they are dark golden brown. Then remove them from the heat, and grind or powder them immediately while they are still warm (whether you do it by hand with a mortar and pestle or in a food processor, they must be *finely* ground). Store in an airtight bottle—keeps well for two weeks or more.

APPETIZERS
AND SNACKS

In Sri Lanka, hors d'oeuvres are unheard of—cooks believe that such tidbits could ruin your appetite for the always-sizable meal that follows.

A more common term for quantities of tasty snacks served with sherry or tea is *short eats*. At parties where these popular finger foods are served, tables may be set with dozens of appetizers that change throughout the evening: patties, Chinese rolls, skewered meats, pork sausages, finger sandwiches, deviled eggs or meats, and countless others.

There's no need to prepare a completely Sri Lankan dinner each time you cook—these aromatic and memorable appetizers can complement a variety of American and European dishes as well. They are delicious for picnics or brunches, as drink accompaniments at parties, or as a light, late-night post-theater meal.

With a Sri Lankan approach to seasoning, ho-hum *rumaki* become delightful and eye-opening, and chutney chicken wings make their American cousins seem a bit one-dimensional. Skewers of meat with spicy peanut sauce (familiar to Americans as *kebabs* in some cultures, *satay* in others) make a perfect pairing with chilled beer or a light wine. Hot, spicy meat *cutlets* ("croquettes") satisfy the partygoer in ways no platter of *crudités* could hope to do. And spicy deviled cashews will forever ruin a nosher's taste for blander nut mixes.

Many of the recipes listed below are ideal brunch items as well: for an unconventional brunch, serve salmon toast or open-face chilies stuffed with salmon. The Sri Lankan deviled crab claws will complement many egg dishes, and stuffed choux

pastry with a variety of fillings—beef, shrimp, or vegetable—plus a fruit salad and champagne make an ideal spring brunch.

BACON AND WATER CHESTNUTS

1 pound bacon (about 15 strips)
1 eight-ounce can (1 cup) water chestnuts
½ teaspoon garlic powder
½ teaspoon chili powder

Wrap each water chestnut with a strip of uncooked bacon, and secure it with a toothpick. Combine the garlic and chili powders, and sprinkle the little bundles of water chestnuts and bacon. Bake at 350°F until golden brown, turning once or twice to cook evenly. You may decrease the chili powder if you prefer a milder flavor. *Serves 6.*

CHICKEN LIVER CANAPÉS

5 chicken livers, boiled
1 hard-boiled egg
½ teaspoon salt
½ teaspoon black pepper
  pinch of garlic powder
  parsley for garnish
2 to 3 tablespoons softened butter
4 to 6 slices of your favorite cocktail-size bread

In a medium-size mixing bowl, mash together the livers and hard-boiled egg. Stir in the salt, pepper, and garlic powder, and blend well. Butter the slices of bread (you may choose to use a cookie cutter and trim the bread into circles), and bake them until golden brown—a few minutes under the broiler. Remove from heat. When they have cooled, spread about 1 teaspoon of the liver mixture on each slice, chill, garnish with a sprig of parsley and serve. *Serves 4.*

CUTLETS (CROQUETTES)

A word about Sri Lankan terminology: Sri Lankans call "croquettes" and "patties" *cutlets*. The Sri Lankan version of a cutlet is a mixture of ground meat, minced seafood, or finely chopped vegetables combined with mashed potatoes, spices, and herbs; Sri Lankan cutlets are formed into balls or patties and usually dipped in beaten egg, then breaded and fried. Their Sinhalese name is *cutlis*.

MEAT CUTLETS

    2 to 3 tablespoons vegetable oil
        1 pound ground meat such as beef, lamb, pork,
          or 2 eight-ounce cans of salmon
          salt and pepper to taste
        2 potatoes, boiled and mashed
       ½ yellow onion, finely chopped
        4 green chilies, finely chopped
        8 curry leaves
        1 teaspoon black pepper
        1 tablespoon lemon juice
        3 eggs, beaten
        2 cups bread crumbs, approximately
        2 cups vegetable oil, approximately, for deep frying

Heat the vegetable oil in a skillet. Sauté the ground meat in the hot oil with salt and pepper to taste until browned. Place the meat (or salmon) in a mixing bowl. Combine with mashed potatoes and chopped onion. Add the chilies, curry leaves, and black pepper, and stir well. Blend in the lemon juice. Form into approximately 25 to 30 one-and-a-half- to two-inch balls. Dip each ball in beaten egg, roll in bread crumbs, and deep-fry in moderately hot oil until golden brown. Drain and serve. *Serves 4 to 6.*

DHAL (LENTIL) CUTLETS

    1 cup dhal (lentils)
    2 cups water
    2 tablespoons vegetable oil
    ½ onion, finely chopped
    6 curry leaves
    1 teaspoon fresh garlic, finely chopped
    ½ teaspoon crushed, dried red chilies
    2 tablespoons crushed Maldive fish
    2 tablespoons crushed, dried shrimp
      pinch of powdered cloves
      pinch of powdered cinnamon
    1 teaspoon lemon juice
      bread crumbs, about ½ cup
    3 eggs, beaten
      vegetable oil for deep frying, about 2 cups

Wash the dhal, and place in a saucepan with 2 cups water. Bring to a boil. Drain off the extra water and mash well. Heat the 2 tablespoons of vegetable oil in a skillet, and sauté the onion, curry leaves, garlic, red chilies, Maldive fish, shrimp, cloves, and cinnamon for about 5 minutes or until the onions are golden brown. Add the dhal and mix well, adding the lemon juice to moisten the mixture. Form the dhal mixture into cutlets (patties) about two inches in diameter. Add bread crumbs as needed if the mixture is too moist. Dip each cutlet in beaten egg and deep-fry in hot oil until golden brown. *Serves 4.*

CUTLETS (PATTIES)

FILLING

¼ pound butter (one stick)
1 four-inch piece rampa
1 five-inch stem lemongrass
4 bay leaves or 12 curry leaves
3 cups boiled chicken, finely chopped
3 cups ground beef
2 cups red onions, finely chopped
½ teaspoon cayenne
½ teaspoon ground cinnamon
½ teaspoon ground cloves
1 teaspoon ground cardamom
4 heaping teaspoons curry powder (optional)
1 six-ounce can (about 1 cup) tomato paste (optional)
4 cups mashed potatoes (optional)

Heat the butter in a saucepan, and brown a quarter cup of the onions, half the rampa, the lemongrass, and four curry leaves. Then add the chicken, the rest of the rampa, the minced beef, and the rest of the onion, spices, and curry leaves. Let it cook over low heat for about 15 minutes. Add tomato paste. Continue to cook until the meat has absorbed the liquids and no gravy is left. Remove the rampa, curry leaves, and lemongrass. Add the mashed potatoes. Mix thoroughly. Cool.

PASTRY

3 cups flour
¾ cup butter (1½ sticks)
6 eggs
   salt to taste
   light cream or whole milk

Melt the butter in a double boiler. Sift the flour, and retain about ½ cup for rolling out the pastry. Combine the salt with the flour, and with your fingers mix in the melted butter. Make a well in the center of the flour, and put in the well-beaten egg yolks. Gradually add enough milk or cream until the mixture forms a stiff paste. Knead lightly until it's smooth, then roll it out on a floured surface. Roll very thin—about ⅛ inch. Cut the dough in circles about 3½ inches in diameter using a can, jar, or cutter. Moisten half of the circle with egg white.

ASSEMBLY

Place a teaspoon of the filling in the middle of each circle, fold the circle in half, and press the edges down together with a fork to seal them. Fry each cutlet in vegetable oil until light golden brown. (You may prefer to brush the cutlets with butter and bake them instead.) Remove and drain well. Makes about 100 cutlets (patties).

CHUTNEY CHICKEN WINGS

> 1 pound chicken wings
> 2 cups vegetable oil, approximately, for frying
> 1 cup cider vinegar
> 1½ cups jaggery (dark or light brown sugar may be substituted)
> 2 tablespoons chili powder
> 2 tablespoons fresh garlic, chopped
> 2 tablespoons fresh gingerroot, minced
> 5 cardamom seeds
> 5 whole cloves
> 1 one-inch piece of cinnamon stick
> 2 teaspoons salt

Heat the vegetable oil in a skillet. Clean the wings (disjoint them if you prefer smaller pieces) and fry until golden brown. Set aside and keep warm. In a saucepan, dissolve the jaggery or sugar in the vinegar over low heat. Cook until it is a thick syrup, then add the chili powder, garlic, ginger, cardamom seeds, cloves, and cinnamon stick. You may adjust the chili powder if you like it more or less fiery. Continue cooking over a low flame. Add the salt and stir continuously so that the mixture doesn't stick to the pan. Cook slowly over low heat for about 20 minutes. Blend the sauce with the wings, coating them thoroughly, and serve hot. The stick cinnamon and cloves are not removed before serving. *Serves 2 to 4.*

Ginger Inguru

CHUTNEY PORK OR BEEF

    1 pound thinly sliced pork, at least 1 to 1½ inches
      thick (or beef ribs)
    2 cups vegetable oil, approximately, for frying
 1½ cups brown sugar
    1 cup cider vinegar
    2 tablespoons chili powder
    2 tablespoons fresh garlic, chopped
    2 tablespoons fresh gingerroot, minced
    5 cardamom seeds
    5 whole cloves
    1 one-inch piece of cinnamon stick
    2 teaspoons salt

Sauté the pork in hot oil until brown. Set aside, and keep warm. Combine the sugar and vinegar in a saucepan and dissolve over low heat. Cook until it is a thick syrup, then add the chili powder, garlic, ginger, cardamom seeds, cloves, and cinnamon stick. You may add more chili powder if you like it more fiery. Continue cooking for about 5 minutes over a low flame. Add salt and stir continuously so that the mixture doesn't stick to the pan. Cook slowly over low heat for about 20 minutes. Remove from the heat while the sauce is still moist. Combine the warm pork and chutney sauce, and serve hot. This dish is also good served cold the next day. *Serves 4 to 6.*

CURRIED PORK ON A STICK,
Easy Method

½ pound thinly sliced pork
1 teaspoon ground cumin
½ teaspoon chili powder
½ teaspoon garlic powder
   salt to taste

Combine the spices and rub into the raw meat until the meat is well coated. Place each strip or piece of pork on a bamboo or metal skewer and grill or broil until golden brown. Serve with peanut sauce for dipping. *Serves 2.*

PEANUT SAUCE

1 cup crunchy peanut butter
2 tablespoons crushed, dried red chilies
½ teaspoon fresh garlic, minced

Blend by hand or in a food processor until smooth. Keeps well in the refrigerator.

DEVILED CASHEWS

　　3　tablespoons butter
　　2　cups raw cashews
　　1　teaspoon chili powder
　½　teaspoon garlic powder
　　1　teaspoon salt (as needed)

Melt the butter, and fry the cashews until they are golden brown. Drain off any excess butter. The Sri Lankan method is to combine the spices and salt on a sheet of white paper and roll the cashews in the seasonings until the nuts are thoroughly coated; it may be easier to use a mixing bowl for this step. Store in an airtight container. Serve as a snack with beer or any other chilled drink.

DEVILED CRAB CLAWS

　　3　tablespoons vegetable oil
　　5　banana chilies
　　1　large yellow onion, sliced
　　2　pounds crab claws, fresh or frozen
　　1　tablespoon curry powder
　　1　tablespoon fresh garlic, minced
　1½　teaspoons fresh gingerroot, finely chopped
　　3　tablespoons crushed, dried red chilies
　½　cup kale, chopped
　　6　curry leaves
　　2　ripe tomatoes, sliced
　　　salt to taste

Heat the oil in a frying pan. When hot, add the banana chilies and sliced onions, and sauté until golden. Add the crab claws, and sprinkle in the curry powder. Add the garlic, ginger, and red chilies, and cook for about 2 minutes. Add the remaining ingredients—kale, curry leaves, and tomatoes. Salt to taste. Cook for about 5 minutes and serve. *Serves 4.*

DEVILED LIVER

        1 pound calves' liver
2 to 3 tablespoons vegetable oil
        1 tablespoon black pepper
           salt to taste
        1 tablespoon fresh garlic, minced
        2 large yellow onions, sliced
        5 large banana chilies, sliced
        2 tablespoons crushed red chilies

Cut liver into bite-size cubes or strips. Heat the vegetable oil in a frying pan. Mix the liver with garlic and black pepper, and fry until it is cooked halfway through. Add the onions, banana chilies, and crushed red chilies, stirring constantly. Add salt to taste. Stir-fry for approximately another 10 minutes over low heat. Tastes great over rice, served with beer. *Serves 4.* *Variation*: Follow the recipe above, but omit the onions. When the liver is cooked, put it on small wooden skewers alternating with pineapple cubes. A good party appetizer.

HOT STUFFED EGGS

        8 hard-boiled eggs
        2 tablespoons tomato sauce
        1 teaspoon chili powder
      ¼ teaspoon garlic powder
        1 heaping tablespoon parsley, finely chopped
        3 tablespoons butter
        3 tablespoons grated cheese (cheddar, colby, or
           American)

Cool the eggs and remove their shells. Cut each egg in half, lengthwise. Scoop out the yolks and place in a mixing bowl. Combine the yolks with the tomato sauce, chili powder, garlic powder, parsley, butter, and cheese. Stuff the egg white halves with the yolk mixture. Chill before serving. *Serves 4.*

MUSHROOM AND BACON APPETIZER

  20 **large fresh mushrooms**
  20 **strips lean bacon**
   1 **teaspoon chili powder**
   1 **teaspoon garlic powder**

Wash the mushrooms, remove the woody tips of their stems, and pat them dry. In a mixing bowl, combine the mushrooms, chili, and garlic, making sure to coat them well. Wrap each mushroom with a strip of bacon, and secure it with a toothpick. Bake or broil until the bacon is crisp. *Serves 4.*

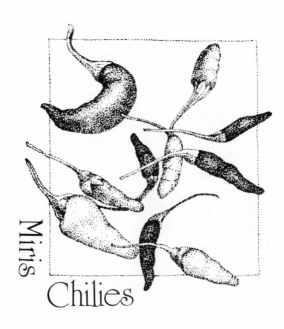

Miris Chilies

COLD OPEN-FACE SALMON-STUFFED CHILIES

1   pound banana chilies
1   eight-ounce can salmon (mackerel or sardines work as well)
½   onion, finely chopped
1   teaspoon garlic, crushed
1   teaspoon black or white pepper
½   cup parsley, finely chopped
1   boiled potato, peeled and mashed

Wash the banana chilies, cut each one in half, and remove the seeds. (If you prefer them very hot, leave in the seeds.) Drain the salmon and discard the liquid. In a mixing bowl, combine the salmon with the remaining ingredients. When the ingredients are thoroughly blended, use fingers or a small spoon to fill each half chili. Some people like a very thin rim of tomato sauce on top of each chili, which tastes great and looks very attractive. *Serves 4. Note*: If you prefer the stuffing cooked, use the same ingredients but brown the onions in hot oil, add the remaining ingredients except the potato, and stir-fry for about 5 minutes. Lastly, add the mashed potato, and mix well before stuffing the banana chili halves.

SALMON TOAST

2 to 3   tablespoons vegetable oil
5   curry leaves
1   onion, chopped
1   eight-ounce can salmon, drained
1   tablespoon parsley, minced
1   tablespoon crushed, dried red chilies
    salt to taste
    a loaf of your favorite bread, sliced
    about ½ stick butter

Heat the oil in a skillet, and brown the onions and curry leaves. Soften the salmon with a fork and add to the skillet. Mix well and cook briefly over low heat, stirring in the parsley, salt, and red chilies. Trim the crusts from the bread, butter the bread lightly, and cut each slice of bread into four squares or strips. Place about 1 teaspoon of the salmon mixture on each piece of bread, and spread with a knife. Place the bread on a cookie sheet, and bake about 20 minutes in a moderate oven (350°F), or until the bread and salmon mixture are toasted golden brown. *Serves 8.*

SHRIMP CANAPÉS

> 2 tablespoons vegetable oil
> 2 cups small cocktail shrimp
> ½ small onion, chopped
> ½ teaspoon fresh garlic, minced
>   salt to taste
> ¼ teaspoon black pepper
> 1 bunch parsley for garnish
> 2 tablespoons horseradish sauce
> 2 to 3 tablespoons butter
> 4 to 6 slices of your favorite thinly sliced cocktail-size bread

Heat the vegetable oil in a medium-size skillet, and brown the shrimp—about 5 minutes. Add the onion, garlic, salt, and pepper. Turn off the heat and allow the mixture to cool. Butter the slices of bread, and then spread each slice with a thin layer of horseradish sauce. Top each slice with the shrimp mixture, and garnish with a sprig of parsley. Chill before serving. *Serves 4. Note:* This dish may also be made with ground beef or lamb instead of shrimp.

STUFFED BANANA CHILIES

  1 pound banana chilies
  2 tablespoons vegetable oil
  ½ pound ground beef or lamb
  1 small onion, chopped
  6 curry leaves
  1 large potato or two medium-size potatoes
1½ teaspoons fresh garlic, minced
1½ teaspoons fresh gingerroot, chopped
  3 cardamom pods, crushed
  1 teaspoon black pepper
  1 teaspoon crushed, dried red chilies
     salt to taste
3 or 4 eggs, beaten
  2 cups bread crumbs, approximately

Banana chilies tend to be hot, so if you like a tamer recipe, remove their seeds before using them. Wash the chilies, make a slit in the middle of each one, and remove the seeds, if desired. (Wash hands well after handling all chilies, and avoid touching your eyes.) Set aside. To make the stuffing, heat the vegetable oil in a skillet, and brown the meat and onion with the curry leaves. Boil the potatoes, mash, and set aside. Add the garlic, ginger, cardamom, black pepper, and red chilies to the meat mixture, and stir over medium heat for about 7 minutes. Salt to taste. Mix in the mashed potatoes. Remove from heat. When the mixture has cooled a bit, use a small spoon or your fingers and stuff each chili, pinching it tightly shut. Dip each stuffed chili in beaten egg, roll it in the bread crumbs, and deep-fry until golden brown. (If the banana chilies are really smooth, the egg and bread crumbs may not stick easily and may need more than one dipping.) *Serves 6.*

STUFFED PUFFS

Choux pastry is a favorite delicacy in Sri Lanka, even though the high heat and humidity render it tricky to make: It can melt before you can get it to the oven! In more temperate climates, however, it should present no problem.

CHOUX PASTRY

½ **cup margarine or butter**
1 **cup water**
1 **cup flour**
4 **eggs**

In a medium-size pan, heat the water and margarine or butter, and bring it to a boil. Gradually stir in the flour, and keep stirring until the mixture forms a ball. Remove from stove, and beat the eggs in one at a time until the mixture is soft and workable. Form one-inch balls, and place about three inches apart on an ungreased cookie sheet. Bake the choux at 350°F until they puff up and turn golden brown. This pastry usually forms a hollow in the center, which is perfect for a variety of stuffings. Slice the top of each pastry puff open, fill by hand or with a teaspoon using the filling of your choice, and close again. *Makes 35 to 40 puffs.*

BEEF STUFFING

2 to 3 tablespoons vegetable oil
½ pound ground beef
1 onion, finely chopped
2 small potatoes, chopped
6 curry leaves
1½ teaspoons fresh garlic, minced
1½ teaspoons fresh gingerroot, minced
½ teaspoon black pepper
½ tablespoon dried, crushed red chilies
 salt to taste

Heat the oil in a skillet, and brown the onions and beef together. Then add the potatoes and fry until brown. Stir in the remaining ingredients except the salt, and cook for about 10 minutes. Add salt to taste. Cool before stuffing the choux. You may want to make this mixture even smoother by using an electric blender or food processor after it has cooled. *Makes enough stuffing for about 30 puffs.*

CANNED FISH STUFFING, *Raw Method*

1 eight-ounce can fish (mackerel or salmon)
½ yellow onion, finely chopped
 a few curry leaves
½ teaspoon black pepper
½ teaspoon fresh garlic, minced
 salt to taste
 juice of one lemon
5 green chilies, finely chopped

Drain the fish and discard the liquid. In a medium-size mixing bowl, combine the fish, herbs and spices, lemon juice, and chilies. Mix well. Using fingers or a small spoon, fill each empty pastry puff with a small amount of the stuffing. The puffs may be warmed again, once filled, or they may be served cold. *Makes enough stuffing for about 2 dozen puffs.*

CANNED FISH STUFFING, *Cooked Method*

1½ tablespoons vegetable oil or butter
 ½ yellow onion, finely chopped
  5 green chilies, chopped
 ½ teaspoon garlic, finely crushed
  6 curry leaves
  1 eight-ounce can fish, drained
 ½ teaspoon black pepper
     juice of 1 lemon
     salt to taste

Heat the oil in a frying pan. Add the onions, green chilies, garlic, and curry leaves, and brown for about 10 minutes. Stir in the fish, mixing it well and breaking it into small pieces with a fork. Add the black pepper, lemon juice, and salt to taste. Cool before use as a stuffing. *Makes enough stuffing for about 2 dozen puffs.*

SHRIMP STUFFING

2 to 3 tablespoons vegetable oil
     1 medium-size yellow onion, finely chopped
     4 ounces dried shrimp (crushed), or 4 ounces fresh or frozen shrimp, finely chopped
     2 potatoes, finely chopped
    ½ teaspoon garlic, finely chopped
    ½ teaspoon fresh gingerroot, minced
   1½ teaspoons curry powder or ground cumin
        a few curry leaves

1 tablespoon crushed, dried red chilies
salt to taste

Heat the oil, and fry the shrimp with the onions over low flame until golden brown. Add the potatoes, and brown. Then add the garlic, ginger, curry powder, curry leaves, and chilies, and stir over low heat for about 10 minutes. Add salt to taste. Remove from heat and cool. Sometimes it's easier to stuff the puffs if the mixture has been blended in an electric blender or food processor after it has cooled. Fill each puff with a small amount of filling. Serve chilled or warm. *Makes enough stuffing for about 30 puffs.*

VEGETABLE STUFFING

2 tablespoons vegetable oil
1 large potato, finely chopped
1 teaspoon fresh garlic, minced
2 teaspoons chili powder
6 curry leaves
1 teaspoon curry powder
½ cup leeks, chopped
½ cup carrots, minced
½ cup cabbage, sliced
½ onion, finely chopped
½ cup spinach leaves, finely chopped
½ cup tomato sauce
salt to taste

Heat the oil in a frying pan. When hot, add the potatoes and fry. Then add spices, stir in the vegetables, and cook until the desired degree of doneness—some cooks prefer it crunchy, others like it soft. Stir in the tomato sauce, and salt to taste. If the vegetables are still too coarse, you may use a food processor to chop the mixture more finely before stuffing the puffs. Serve chilled or warm. *Makes enough stuffing for about 2 dozen puffs.*

CHAPTER 8

THE (HOT) STAFF OF LIFE

Rottis, Hoppers, and Pittu

ROTTIS

Rottis (row´ tees), a pan-fried soft bread, are similar to Indian flat breads such as *nan* and look a lot like Scandinavian *lefse*, but the Sri Lankan versions sometimes contain fresh grated coconut or, if that's not available, desiccated (dry) coconut. Sri Lankans usually serve them with curries and sambols, and they are very popular for breakfast in Sri Lanka. Rottis can be wrapped around meat or vegetable mixtures, or they can be torn with the fingers and dipped into curries and sambols.

Sri Lankans love rottis with beer, and they may be eaten alone or as a side dish. Coconut rottis are typically eaten for breakfast, but once in a while Sri Lankans crave them for supper with a hot meat curry and *lunumiris*, a sambol made with crushed, red chilies and onion. Restaurants rarely serve rottis, although you will find rotti vendors on the streets; it's not uncommon for people to take two dozen rottis home from a "take away" (take-out) shop.

Small rottis can be served as a side dish, larger ones as a main course. The thickness of the dough can vary, too. However, novice rotti makers may find that their thin rottis will break. It's best to practice making your first batches in a fairly hefty weight and gradually work up to handling the dough and stretching it to a more delicate thinness. Rottis are, frankly, deceptively tricky to make; some people practice for years to get the right consistency.

COCONUT ROTTI

   2 cups flour (roasted rice flour, unbleached flour, or regular all-purpose flour)
½ cup desiccated coconut
     salt to taste (about 1 teaspoon)
   1 cup water, approximately (just enough to moisten the dough)
     vegetable oil

In a large mixing bowl, mix flour, coconut, and salt. Add enough warm water to make a soft dough. Knead it until it forms a ball and does not stick to the sides of the bowl. Shape it into balls about 2 inches in diameter. Then flatten each ball on a greased plate or cutting surface, spreading it until it is as thin or thick as desired. Fry on a dry preheated griddle until golden brown on both sides. *Serves 4.*

FANCY COCONUT ROTTI

   3 cups flour
   1 cup desiccated coconut
   6 curry leaves
   2 tablespoons crushed dried shrimp
½ onion, chopped
10 green chilies, chopped

1 cup warm water, approximately (just enough to
   moisten the dough)
   vegetable oil

Combine the ingredients, and follow the procedure for coconut rotti above. But before frying, fill with the following:

FILLING

½ cup green onion or leeks, finely chopped
1 teaspoon crushed, dried red chilies
½ cup cabbage, finely chopped
½ cup kale, finely chopped
   a few curry leaves (optional)
   salt
   black pepper
   vegetable oil for frying

In a bowl, combine the green onions or leeks, red chilies,
cabbage, kale, and curry leaves. Add salt and pepper to taste.
Heat the oil in a skillet, and sauté the vegetables and spices
until golden. Place about 2 tablespoons of the filling on each
rotti, fold the rotti in half, and pinch the edges together to form
a packet enclosing the vegetables. Heat the vegetable oil in a
skillet, and fry each rotti until the filling is warmed through.
Serves 4.

GOTHAMBER ROTTI

3 cups unbleached flour
   salt to taste
   hot water
   enough vegetable oil to cover the rotti balls and
   soak them

This dish is best when mixed in a food processor, but you
may also try hand mixing. Put the flour and salt in a mixing bowl,

and add water a little at a time until the dough becomes soft and pliable. Add flour to prevent sticking, if needed. Form into balls about 2 inches in diameter. Soak covered in vegetable oil for least 3 hours, then flatten out by hand or rolling pin on a well-greased cutting board until they are as thin as possible. Griddle-fry until golden. *Serves 6.*

FILLING

> ⅜ cup onions, chopped
> 2 to 3 green chilies, diced
> ¼ cup crushed dried shrimp
>   bread crumbs
>   vegetable oil for frying

In a separate bowl, combine the chopped onions, green chilies, and crushed dried shrimp. Sauté in a skillet in hot oil until golden. Add ½ teaspoon curry powder if you prefer it spicier. Remove a rotti dough ball from the oil, and flatten it on a greased cutting board into a circle. Place about 2 tablespoons of stuffing in the center of the dough and fold over the edges, like a burrito or crepe, until the edges are well-tucked around the filling. Then roll the packet lightly in bread crumbs, and fry until golden brown. Repeat the process with each ball of dough. *Serves 6 to 8.*

PLAIN ROTTI WITH MEAT, FISH, OR VEGETABLES

> 3 to 4 tablespoons vegetable oil
> 2 tablespoons chopped onions
> 2 green chilies, chopped
> ½ cup ground meat, minced fish, or any mixture of chopped vegetables (leeks, small chopped potatoes, carrots, and cabbage)
>   salt and pepper to taste

2 rotti dough balls (see previous recipe,
    Gothamber Rotti)

Heat the vegetable oil in a skillet. Add the chopped onions
and chilies, then stir in the minced meat or fish, salt, and pepper.
Set aside. Flatten the rotti dough balls into a round shape on a
greased paper or greased surface. Stuff as described in previous
recipe. Bake on a greased baking sheet at about 350°F until
golden brown. *Serves 2.*

ROTTIS WITH PRAWN STUFFING

3 to 4	tablespoons vegetable oil
8	large prawns, chopped
½	cup leeks, chopped
½	cup cabbage, sliced
1½	teaspoons chili powder
½	cup carrots, sliced
½	cup boiled dhal (lentils)
½	teaspoon fresh garlic, minced
½	teaspoon fresh gingerroot, chopped
1	teaspoon ground cumin
	salt to taste
2	cups bread crumbs, approximately
	more vegetable oil, approximately 2 cups, for frying
4 to 6	Gothamber rotti dough balls

Heat the oil in a skillet and brown the prawns. Add the leeks,
cabbage, chili powder, carrots, dhal, garlic, ginger, and cumin.
Fry for a few minutes, then add salt to taste, and cook until the
vegetables are done to your liking. Set aside to cool. To stuff
the rottis, flatten out the raw rotti dough ball into a circle on a
very smooth cutting board, then place a big tablespoonful or
two of the stuffing in the center. Tuck in two ends and fold the
rotti dough, rolling it like a Chinese egg roll. Dip the stuffed

rotti in bread crumbs (the oil from the soaking will help retain the bread crumbs), and deep-fry until golden. *Serves 4.*

ROTTIS WITH LAMB STUFFING

      2 tablespoons vegetable oil
      2 cups lamb, chopped or diced (leftover cooked
        lamb may be used)
 1½ teaspoons fresh garlic, minced
      ½ teaspoon fresh gingerroot, chopped
      1 tablespoon curry powder
      1 teaspoon chili powder
      ½ cup onion, chopped
      4 green chilies, chopped
      2 cups spinach leaves, chopped
      ½ cup carrots, chopped
      ½ cup sliced cabbage
        salt to taste
 4 to 6 Gothamber rotti dough balls

Heat the oil and brown the lamb, stirring in the garlic, ginger, curry powder, and chili powder. Add the remaining vegetables and the green chilies, and brown for about 5 minutes or until vegetables have reached the desired firmness. Salt to taste. Cool before stuffing the rottis using the method described for Prawn Stuffing. *Serves 4.*

ROTTIS WITH VEGETABLE STUFFING

      1 cup dhal (lentils)
      2 tablespoons vegetable oil
      ½ cup onions, chopped
      ½ teaspoon fresh garlic, minced
      ½ teaspoon fresh gingerroot, chopped
      2 teaspoons crushed, dried red chilies

1½ teaspoons coriander
1½ teaspoons ground cumin (or curry powder)
½ cup cabbage, sliced
½ cup broccoli, chopped
½ cup leeks, chopped
½ cup carrots, minced
½ cup kale, finely chopped
   salt to taste

Wash the dhal, and soak it covered in warm water over low heat for about 1 hour; then set aside. Heat the oil in a skillet. When the oil is hot, add the dhal, onions, garlic, and ginger, and then brown until golden. Lower the heat, and add the red chilies, cumin, and coriander. Cook for about 2 minutes, stirring constantly. Then add the vegetables. Salt to taste and cook to desired crispness. Stuff the rottis, using the method described for Prawn Stuffing, and deep-fry. *Serves 4.*

HOPPERS

Hoppers are somewhat similar to crepes or pancakes. Traditionally, hoppers were eaten for breakfast and snacks. They are eaten in Sri Lanka with sambols, with sweetening such as honey or syrup, or with butter and jam. Originally, palm toddy was used for leavening in hoppers, but this has been replaced by yeast.

Rice flour is traditional for the hopper, and gives a better result than the self-rising flour. The batter needs to ferment overnight. It must then be thinned with coconut milk before cooking. The result looks something like a crepe before it's folded, with air holes in it like in an English muffin. The word itself comes from the Tamil *appam* or *apu*, which means "clapping with the hands"; and that is how hoppers are shaped.

Traditionally, hoppers were made in hopper pans that were made of iron and shaped like a miniature wok. You may find them in oriental food stores, or you may use any bowl-shaped pan to fry your hoppers, just so the edges get crisp and the middle is still thick. Hoppers, pittu, or tempered (sautéed, leftover) rice are standard breakfast fare.

I have not included a recipe for a variation of hopper called *string hopper* in which little "strings," or threads, of dough are filtered through special pans onto a hot greased pan and then steamed, because such pans are unlikely to be available in the West. But sometime if a Sri Lankan family invites you home to try them, don't decline the opportunity—string hoppers are delicious.

In Sri Lanka, a whole class of specialists make up string and egg hoppers to "take away" (take out). Where I lived on Rodney Street in Borella, a neighborhood of Colombo, there was a section of huts where very poor people lived. Their kitchens were smaller than our bathrooms here in the States and the ceilings so low you that you had to duck to enter them. But inside, old Sinhalese women would make you the *best* breakfast in the world! They made egg hoppers, string hoppers, plain hoppers, and sambols with them—at the time, the price was about a nickel apiece and I could easily eat six. If you brought your own eggs, the hoppers would be even cheaper! The woman would have a little iron pan on the fire; she'd take a cloth with grease on it, rub a one-cent piece with the grease, and coat the pan. I can still remember the dull ringing sound of the metal against metal very well. Then she'd take a heaping cup of batter and pour it in, and in only about a minute out came the hopper. The women also provided curries and gravies; you never knew exactly what was in them, but they were the best hoppers anywhere.

EGG HOPPERS

4 **cups self-rising flour**
2 **cups milk**
1 **cup water**
3 **eggs**
2 **tablespoons sugar**
 salt to taste

Combine the flour, milk, and water, and mix well until thick. Stir in the eggs, sugar, and salt. Mix well with an electric beater for 10 to 15 minutes. Cover the dough with a cloth dish towel, and allow it to sit for 20 minutes. Heat the hopper pan, and oil it. Pour a heaping tablespoon of hopper batter in the middle of the hot pan, and turn to coat the pan as you would a crepe. The middle of the dough will be thick, and the sides will remain crispy. Break an egg and place it in the middle of the hopper. When the egg is cooked, the hopper is done. It's always eaten with a hot curry and a sambol—sort of the Egg McMuffin of Sri Lanka. *Depending on the amount of batter used for each one, makes a dozen or more hoppers.*

PLAIN HOPPERS

  2 cups lightly roasted rice flour
¾ cup coconut water (the juice drained from an
     opened coconut)
  1 cup coconut milk
  1 cup diluted coconut milk, if needed to thin the batter
  1 teaspoon baking soda

Mix the flour with baking soda, and stir in the coconut water.
Knead it well. Allow it to stand overnight, covered with a clean
dish towel. A few hours before making the hoppers, add the
coconut milk, a little at a time. Cover it and allow it to sit 30
minutes. Preheat a small wok (the deeper the better). You may
need to grease the skillet with butter—real hopper pans don't
stick—or use a nonstick pan. Pour half a cup of batter in the
middle of the pan, and swirl it around to spread the batter—
just as you would in making a crepe. Cover and cook over low
heat for a minute or more. When the edges are crisp, lift the
hopper up with a spatula. (If the mixture is too thick when you
start to fry it, add a little more thin coconut milk.) *Makes 8 to
10 small to medium hoppers.* (One can easily eat five hoppers
at dinner.)

pol
Coconut

INSTANT HOPPERS, *Easy Method*

4 cups self-rising flour
2 cups milk
1 cup water
3 eggs
2 tablespoons sugar
   salt to taste

Add the milk and water to the flour, and mix well until the mixture is thick. Add the eggs, sugar, and salt. Mix well with electric beater for 10 to 15 minutes. Cover with a dish towel and let it sit. The mixture should be ready for use in about 20 minutes. Pour a heaping tablespoon of hopper batter in the middle of a hot pan, and swirl it about the pan like a crepe to spread the batter. The middle of the dough will be thick, and the sides will remain crispy. *Makes approximately 6 hoppers.*

PITTU

Pittu has no analogy in Western cooking. It replaces bread, rice, or rotti in a meal, and is typically eaten for breakfast, but many people like it for dinner.

In Sri Lanka, there are special bamboo pittu molds tied with string that aren't available in the United States. But a small, round bamboo or metal steamer of the kind used to steam vegetables in a wok makes an acceptable substitute. For traditional flavor, texture, and appearance, rice flour is best, but if it's not available, you may use regular white flour.

To steam it properly, pack the raw dough into the steamer tightly—this should form a solid cake. After it's steamed, flip it over on a plate and slice it or break it up with your hands.

Or if the dough is not sufficient to fill the container snugly, simply steam it as is, and allow the mixture to be loose, served hot and crumbly like rice.

RICE FLOUR PITTU

⅜ cup (6 tablespoons) coconut milk
2 cups desiccated coconut
1 pound rice flour
salt to taste (about 1 teaspoon)
water as needed

Combine flour, coconut, and salt in a large mixing bowl. Using your fingers, mix them well. Add half the coconut milk and work the mixture until the ingredients form little ball-shaped grains, adding a few drops of water as necessary. Steam the pittu dough in a round steamer for about 25 minutes. While it is still hot, remove from steamer onto serving plate and pour the other half of the coconut milk over it. Serve it hot with a curry and a hot sambol. *Serves 4 to 6.*

CHAPTER 9

MAIN COURSES
Beef, Chicken, Fish, Lamb, Pork, Shellfish, and Vegetarian Dishes

It's not unusual to go to a Sri Lankan home for dinner and have as many as twenty main-course dishes spread out before you. And you're supposed to taste it all!

It's part of tradition for guests to eat and then eat more, or the hosts will be hurt—if not insulted! Fortunately, the hot climate and the amount of walking many Sri Lankans do helps to control weight gain, as does the fact that the majority of dishes are vegetarian.

But the big meals are linked to the Sri Lankan ideal of beauty: Once married, women are *expected* to get a bit round. For decades, nobody in the leisure classes exercised—why bother attaining leisure-class status if you had to pound, sweat, and thrash it off? In the last five years or so, however, a bit of Western-inspired weight-and-fitness consciousness has infiltrated the thinking of younger Sri Lankans. So both the standard of beauty and the twenty-entrée dinners may be in for a change.

For all but the poor, rice is only a lunch meal. A typical dinner for the middle class (the heaviest meal of the day, eaten at 8 p.m. or so) might consist of rice, dhal, beans, potatoes, eggplant, steamed mallung, one or two meat or fish curries, and onion sambol or chutney. Sri Lankans often include fresh greens in their meals called *gotu kola* and *mukunu wenna*.

The former is thought to help thicken the hair and keep the skin looking young, while the latter is supposed to keep the eyes bright and strong.

BEEF
KUDU BADUM (BEEF CURRY)

- 1 pound (2 cups) beef, cubed (fresh or leftover tenderloin, stew, or steak meat may be used)
- 1 one-inch piece cinnamon stick
- 1 two-inch piece rampa
- 1 one-inch piece lemongrass
- 8 curry leaves
- 1 teaspoon fresh garlic, minced
- 1 teaspoon gingerroot, crushed
- ½ onion, chopped
- ¼ cup vinegar
  salt to taste
- 1½ cups water
- 3 tablespoons vegetable oil
- 1½ tablespoons chili powder (you may use paprika if you don't like it spicy hot)
- 1½ tablespoons curry powder
- 2 cups coconut milk

In a large skillet, combine the meat with the other ingredients except the oil, chili powder, curry powder, and coconut milk. Cook over medium heat until all the water has been absorbed. Then add the vegetable oil, and stir-fry the beef for about 3 minutes. Add the curry powder and chili powder (you may substitute paprika) and continue stirring for 3 minutes. Add a bit more oil if needed. Lastly, add the coconut milk, and simmer gently for a few minutes more. *Serves 4.*

BEEF CUTLETS (CROQUETTES)

Hot, spicy, and satisfying, cutlets may serve as an appetizer or entrée: This is an entrée-size version of the appetizer cutlets in Chapter 7.

        3 to 4 tablespoons vegetable oil
            1 pound ground beef
        1½ teaspoons salt
            4 green chilies
            1 sprig of parsley, finely chopped
            1 teaspoon black pepper
            ½ large onion, finely chopped
            4 potatoes, cooked and mashed
        3 to 4 beaten eggs
                bread crumbs
                vegetable oil for frying

Heat the vegetable oil in a saucepan, and add the meat, salt, green chilies, parsley, and black pepper. Sauté until golden; then stir in the chopped onion. Remove from heat and cool. Add the mashed potatoes and mix well. Divide into about 16 portions, forming balls or flat cutlets. Dip each ball or cutlet into beaten egg, then into bread crumbs. Deep-fry until golden brown. *Serves 4.*

BEEF SATHI CURRY*

   1 pound (2 cups) beef, cubed
   2 teaspoons ground black pepper
  ¼ cup cider vinegar
   3 cloves fresh garlic, sliced
   2 one-inch pieces gingerroot, peeled and sliced
   8 curry leaves
   3 one-inch pieces rampa
   1 two-inch piece lemongrass
      salt to taste
   2 cups water, approximately
3 to 4 tablespoons vegetable oil
  ½ onion, sliced
   1 teaspoon saffron
   2 cups coconut milk
      juice of one lime or lemon
   2 tablespoons flour (optional)

Place the beef in a saucepan. Add the pepper, vinegar, garlic, ginger, half the curry leaves, rampa, lemongrass, and salt. Add about 1 cup of the water, and cook until the beef is tender and the water is absorbed. Then add the oil and sauté the beef until brown. Set aside. In another pan, place the remaining curry leaves, rampa, lemongrass, saffron, onions, and coconut milk. Salt to taste, and cook, stirring constantly, for about 10 minutes. Then add the lemon or lime juice. Add the beef to this pan, and cook for a minute or two over medium heat. You may add 2 tablespoons flour to make the gravy thicker if you prefer. *Serves 4.*

*Sathi Curry is similar to *satay*, a dish found in Malaysia, Japan, and Indonesia.

BEEF TONGUE STEW

        1 pound beef tongue, cubed
      ¼ cup cider vinegar
        1 teaspoon saffron
        1 tablespoon black peppercorns
    1½ tablespoons curry powder
          salt to taste
        1 cup water
        1 cup potatoes, cut into large cubes
      ½ cup carrots, cubed
      ½ cup green beans, chopped
        2 large onions, chopped
      ½ cup cabbage, coarsely chopped
        1 cup milk
        2 tablespoons flour

Place the tongue in a pot with the vinegar, saffron, peppercorns, and curry powder. Salt to taste. Add the cup of water and
bring to a boil over low heat. When it is half-cooked (about 15
minutes), add the potatoes, carrots, and beans, and cook for
about 5 minutes over medium heat. Then add the onions and
cabbage, and cook 5 more minutes. Add the milk and cook for
another 10 minutes. Stir in 2 tablespoons flour to thicken the
juice. This should take about 2 or 3 minutes. *Serves 4.*

CEYLON BEEF CURRY

        2 tablespoons vegetable oil
      ¼ cup onions, chopped
        2 cloves garlic, minced
        1 one-inch piece gingerroot, crushed
        8 curry leaves
        2 pounds beef, cubed
        2 tablespoons curry powder
        1 tablespoon crushed, dried red chilies

3 one-inch pieces rampa
  a pinch of lemongrass
2 cups coconut milk, regular milk, or light cream
  salt to taste
  the juice of one lime

Heat the vegetable oil in a pan and sauté the onions, garlic, ginger, and curry leaves until golden brown. Add the cubed beef and the remaining spices, and stir for about 10 minutes. Add the milk and add salt to taste. Cook over low heat until the gravy is thickened. Add the lime juice and cook for about 2 minutes. *Serves 4.*

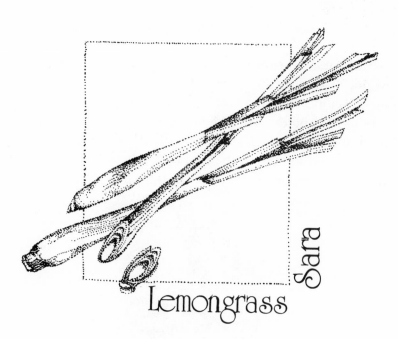

Lemongrass Sara

DEVILED LIVER AND ONIONS

2 tablespoons vegetable oil
1 tablespoon fresh garlic, chopped
1 pound calves' liver, thinly sliced
1 half-inch piece stick cinnamon
5 cardamom pods, crushed
8 curry leaves
3 large onions, sliced
6 banana chilies, sliced
1 large ripe tomato, sliced
1 tablespoon crushed black peppercorns
½ teaspoon curry powder
  salt to taste
1 tablespoon crushed, dried red chilies (optional)

Heat the vegetable oil in a pan. When hot, add the garlic. Then add the liver and fry until almost crisp. (You may need more oil.) Add the cinnamon, cardamom, and curry leaves, and cook for 1 minute. Stir in the sliced onions and the banana chilies. Continue cooking over medium heat, stirring constantly, for about 10 minutes, then add the tomato. Sprinkle in the black pepper and curry powder. Salt to taste. If you prefer this dish very spicy, add the crushed, dried red chilies. Cook for about 5 more minutes. *Serves 4 to 6.*

MUSTARD BEEF CURRY

½ cup brown mustard seeds
¼ cup cider vinegar
¼ cup vegetable oil
½ large onion, chopped
⅜ cup garlic, minced (about 8 large cloves)
⅜ cup fresh gingerroot, finely chopped
1½ tablespoons curry powder
2 pounds beef, cubed (use round steak, sirloin, or stew meat)
4 whole cloves
4 cardamom pods, crushed
½ cinnamon stick
½ tablespoon turmeric
1 tablespoon ground black pepper
8 curry leaves
2 cups water
salt to taste

Put the mustard seeds, vinegar, and a dash of water into a blender, and blend until all the seeds are crushed. Set aside. (If you do not have brown mustard seeds, you may substitute semiground, bottled Ingelhoffer mustard or any whole-grain mustard except the Dijon type.) Heat the oil in a large skillet, and brown the onions, garlic, and ginger. Add the curry powder and beef, and stir over medium heat until browned—about 5 minutes. Stir in the cloves, cardamom, cinnamon stick, turmeric, black pepper, and curry leaves. Add the water and the mustard-seed blend, and stir well. Simmer until the sauce is thick. Serve with rice or noodles. *Serves 4 to 6.*

CHICKEN

CHICKEN CURRY (KUKAL MAS),
Easy Method

       2 pounds (4 cups) chicken, cut up
     ½ large onion, chopped
     ½ cup celery, chopped
     ¼ cup garlic, chopped
     ¼ cup fresh gingerroot, minced
       1 teaspoon each turmeric, coriander, cumin, and
          chili powder
       4 whole cloves
       4 cardamom pods, crushed
     ½ cup soy sauce
    1½ tablespoons cider vinegar
       2 cups milk, water, or coconut milk
       1 three-inch cinnamon stick
          salt to taste
       8 curry leaves
       2 one-inch pieces lemongrass
       3 one-inch pieces rampa

Combine the onions, celery, garlic, ginger, turmeric, coriander, cumin, chili powder, cloves, cardamom seeds, soy sauce,
and cider vinegar. Rub the chicken well with the mixture, and
marinate several hours or overnight. Place the chicken and the
marinade in a medium-size kettle, add the milk or water, cinnamon stick, salt, curry leaves, lemongrass, and rampa, and cook
on low heat for about 1 hour or until chicken is done. Serve
the chicken in its sauce together with rice and a sambol, a green
vegetable curry, or dhal. *Serves 4.*

CHICKEN MULLIGATAWNY SOUP

        1 pound (2 cups) chicken, bones and all, cut into
          small portions
 4 to 6 cups water
      ½ teaspoon salt
        1 teaspoon black pepper
        1 tablespoon ground coriander
      ½ tablespoon ground cumin
          pinch of saffron
        2 large ripe tomatoes, sliced
        1 onion, sliced
        2 one-inch pieces cinnamon stick
      ½ teaspoon fresh gingerroot, chopped
      ½ teaspoon fresh garlic, minced
        2 tablespoons vegetable oil
       10 curry leaves
        2 cups coconut milk
        2 tablespoons lemon juice

Put the chicken and water into a large saucepan, and bring to a boil. Add salt, pepper, coriander, cumin, saffron, sliced tomatoes, half the onions, stick cinnamon, ginger, and garlic. Simmer for 30 minutes. Remove from heat. In a skillet, heat the vegetable oil, and brown the rest of the onions and the curry leaves. When brown, add the coconut milk. Then add to the chicken mixture. Return the saucepan to the heat, and add the lemon juice. Bring it to a boil and simmer 15 minutes. Serve hot, over rice if you prefer. *Serves 4.*

CURRIED CHICKEN WITH NOODLES

¼ cup vegetable oil or margarine
½ large onion, coarsely chopped
1 tablespoon fresh garlic, minced
1 tablespoon fresh gingerroot, finely chopped
1 pound chicken cut up into small portions, with or without bones
1½ teaspoons ground cumin
1½ teaspoons ground coriander
1 teaspoon chili powder
8 curry leaves
an inch or two of lemongrass (optional)
1 cup water
1 bunch green onions, sliced
1 cup cabbage, coarsely chopped
½ cup any fresh green vegetable such as kale or broccoli, chopped
about 1 cup of any Chinese presteamed noodles

In a wide saucepan or frying pan, brown the onions in the vegetable oil, and then add the garlic and ginger. Add the chicken, and fry until the pieces are lightly browned. Then add the cumin, coriander, chili powder, and curry leaves and the lemongrass if you wish. Add the water, and cook over low heat until the chicken is cooked through (about 10 minutes). Finally, fold in the green onions, cabbage, green vegetables, and the noodles. If there's not enough gravy, add water or milk. Cook an additional 10 minutes. *Serves 4.*

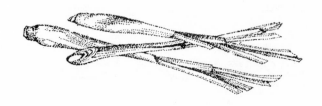

TEMPERED* CHICKEN CURRY

- ½ cup vegetable oil or butter
- ½ large onion, coarsely chopped
- ½ cup celery, chopped
  about ⅛ cup each fresh gingerroot and garlic, crushed
- 8 curry leaves
- 3 one-inch pieces rampa
- 1 two-inch piece lemongrass
- 4 whole cloves
- 4 cardamom pods, crushed
- 1 cinnamon stick
- 1 tablespoon ground coriander
- 1 tablespoon ground cumin
- 1 teaspoon turmeric
- 1½ teaspoons cider vinegar
- 1 tablespoon chili powder
- 2 pounds chicken, cut up
- ½ cup soy sauce
  salt to taste

Heat the oil in a medium-size frying pan, and brown the onion, celery, ginger, garlic, curry leaves, rampa, and lemongrass. Then add the cloves, cardamom, and cinnamon stick. Turn the heat down, and add the coriander, cumin, turmeric, vinegar, and chili powder until the mixture is lightly browned. Add the cut-up chicken, and stir into mixture. Add soy sauce, salt to taste, and cook over low heat. To make additional gravy, add 2 cups water or 1 cup water and 1 cup coconut milk. If you prefer to make this or any other meat curry only mildly spicy, do not add the chili powder; add more of course, if you like it hotter. *Serves 4 to 6.*

*Tempered is a Sinhalese style of cooking; it means either sautéed or stir-fried.

WHITE CHICKEN CURRY
WITH POTATOES

3 to 4 tablespoons ghee or any cooking oil
  ½ onion, chopped
  3 green chilies, finely chopped
  1 tablespoon black pepper
  1 tablespoon ground cumin
  2 teaspoons turmeric
  6 curry leaves
  1 tablespoon fresh garlic, minced
  1 tablespoon fresh gingerroot, chopped
  1 pound chicken, cut up
  4 large potatoes, washed and cubed
  ½ teaspoon fennel seed (optional)
  2 cups water
  1 cup milk

In a large skillet, heat the oil, and brown the onion and green chilies. Add the black pepper, cumin, turmeric, curry leaves, garlic, and ginger. Then add the chicken, potatoes, fennel seed, and two cups water. Simmer until the potatoes and chicken are tender. As the sauce cooks, it will evaporate; so add a cup of milk 10 minutes before you are done and simmer over low heat so the milk sauce does not boil over. Serve with rice, one green vegetable, and a sambol. *Serves 4.*

FISH

FISH CURRY (AMBUL THIAL)

> 2 pounds (4 cups) tuna or any firm, fresh fish (mackerel, marlin, or sardines)
> 2 tablespoons lemon juice
>   a sprinkle of salt
> 1 tablespoon ground black pepper
> 2 tablespoons chili powder
> 1 teaspoon fresh ginger, chopped
> 12 curry leaves
> 6 pieces goraka (optional) or 3 large tomatoes crushed with 1 tablespoon cider vinegar
>   about 1 cup water

Wash the fish, and cut it into large pieces (leaving on the skin and bones). Rub each piece with a little lemon juice. Goraka is usually tough; boil it until it is soft and then crush it up. (If you can't find goraka, substitute tomatoes marinated briefly in cider vinegar.) Combine all vegetable and spice ingredients and water in a pot, and then add the fish. Simmer on low heat until almost all the juices are gone, turning the fish once to make sure the spices and juices penetrate both sides evenly. Serve with rice. This dish can be quite spicy and will have a tart taste. *Serves 4.*

SALMON OR FISH CURRY

    2 to 3 tablespoons vegetable oil or butter
    ½ onion, chopped
    3 or 4 one-inch pieces lemongrass
       3 cloves of garlic, minced
       1 one-inch piece cinnamon stick
       1 teaspoon chili powder
       2 cups milk
       1 teaspoon ground turmeric
         salt to taste
       2 eight-ounce cans salmon or other fish such as
         mackerel (fresh fish is fine as well)
       1 tablespoon lemon juice

Heat the oil in a medium-size skillet, and brown the onions. Reduce the heat, and add the lemongrass, garlic, cinnamon stick, and chili powder. Add the milk and turmeric. Salt to taste, and cook over low heat for about 2 minutes. Add the fish, keeping the heat low so the milk doesn't curdle, and cook until the fish flakes easily. If the fish is precooked you don't need to cook it very long—just enough to bring it to a boil. You may add need to add more water. Finally, add the lemon juice. *Serves 4.*

DRY-FISH CURRY

    2 tablespoons vegetable oil
    ½ large onion, sliced
    1 teaspoon fresh garlic, minced
    6 curry leaves
    ½ cinnamon stick
    1 teaspoon chili powder
    1 tablespoon ground cumin
    ¼ teaspoon ground turmeric
    1 cup water
    1 cup milk

pinch lemongrass
about 4 pieces of goraka or two tomatoes (optional)
salt to taste

1 tablespoon lemon juice
½ pound dried salted fish such as tuna, or frozen dried codfish

Heat the vegetable oil in a large skillet. Brown the onion, garlic, curry leaves, and cinnamon stick. Stir in the chili powder, cumin, and turmeric. Then pour in the water and milk. Salt to taste, but do so sparingly since the fish is already salted. Add the remaining ingredients and the fish, and simmer for about 10 minutes. Serve with rice and one or two other vegetable dishes. *Serves 4.*

FISH AND TOMATO STEW

2 to 3 tablespoons vegetable oil
  1 pound (2 cups) any fresh, firm fish (tuna, halibut, etc.) cut into one- or two-inch cubes
 1½ medium onions, chopped
  1 teaspoon fresh garlic, minced
  1 teaspoon fresh gingerroot, finely chopped
  5 banana chilies, sliced
 10 curry leaves
  3 cardamom pods, crushed
  2 tablespoons ground mustard seed
  1 teaspoon ground black pepper
  1 cup water
  3 large tomatoes, sliced
  1 teaspoon salt (or salt to taste)
  1 tablespoon lemon juice

Heat the vegetable oil in a large frying pan, and lightly sauté the fish cubes on both sides. Remove them from the pan and set aside. To the same oil, add sliced onions, garlic, ginger, banana chilies, curry leaves, and cardamom pods, and brown for about 5 minutes. Then stir in the mustard seed and black pepper. Add a cup of water. Stir well, making sure the mustard is well mixed with the other ingredients. Then add the tomatoes and fish, and coat them well with the vegetable-and-spice blend, stirring gently so the fish stays intact. Add the salt and lemon juice, and simmer for about 15 minutes or until the fish and spicy tomato sauce is done to your liking. *Serves 4.*

FISH CUTLETS (CROQUETTES)

        4 potatoes
        1 pound (2 cups) of any boiled, boneless fish
          (canned fish will do)
      ½ teaspoon ground cumin
      ½ teaspoon ground black pepper
      ½ large onion, finely chopped
        3 green chilies, finely chopped
       10 curry leaves
   3 or 4 eggs, well beaten
          bread crumbs
          vegetable oil sufficient to deep-fry the cutlets

Boil the potatoes until soft, drain, and place in a medium-size mixing bowl. Add the fish, spices, onion, chilies, and curry leaves. Mix well, crushing the mixture together, then separate it into ten to fifteen portions. Shape each portion into round balls and flatten the ball into a cutlet (patty). Dip in beaten egg and then in bread crumbs, and fry in hot oil until golden brown. Great with beer. *Serves 4.*

FISH WITH GINGER SAUCE

 ½ cup coconut treacle or maple syrup
2 to 3 tablespoons flour
 1 pound (2 cups) any firm fish, cubed
 3 tablespoons finely minced fresh gingerroot or
 ginger preserve
 1 cup pineapple juice
 2 tablespoons soy sauce
 1 small cucumber, cubed
 3 banana chilies, sliced in rings
 2 ripe tomatoes, sliced
 salt to taste

Heat the treacle or maple syrup in a skillet. Lightly flour the fish cubes, and add them to the hot syrup. When the syrup starts

to bubble, turn the fish over. In a separate saucepan, combine the ginger, pineapple juice, and soy sauce, and bring to a boil. Add the remaining flour and mix well. Simmer for 5 minutes. Stir in the cucumber, banana chilies, and tomato, and cook for a minute or two. Add salt to taste. Combine this with the sautéed fish, and cook another minute, until the fish is warmed through. Serve over rice. *Serves 4.*

FISH STEAK CURRY

    4 fish steaks such as marlin, shark, salmon, mahi mahi,
      halibut (you may substitute 4 whole medium-small
      fish such as trout cleaned and with heads and tails
      removed)
    2 tablespoons lemon juice
      sprinkle of salt
    ¼ cup vegetable oil
    1 tablespoon fresh garlic, crushed
    1 tablespoon crushed mustard seeds or Ingelhoffer
      bottled mustard (or any whole-grain mustard)
    ½ teaspoon chili powder
    ½ teaspoon curry powder
    1 cup water
    1 cup coconut milk
    ½ onion, sliced

Wash and clean the fish steaks, sprinkle with salt and lemon juice. Heat half the vegetable oil in a skillet, and brown the fish until golden. Heat oil in a second pan, and combine all remaining ingredients except onions, stirring well. Add the onions to the fish and brown them. Then add the sauce mixture, and simmer until the fish flakes easily. *Serves 4.*

FRIED FISH CURRY

>   1   pound (2 cups) any firm fresh fish, cut into inch-
>   thick slices
> ½   teaspoon saffron
>   a sprinkle of salt and black pepper
> 2 to 3 tablespoons vegetable oil
>   1   onion, sliced
>   3   green chilies, chopped
>   2   teaspoons cumin seeds
>   2   cups coconut milk or light cream
>   3   cloves fresh garlic, minced
>   1   one-inch piece rampa
>   10   curry leaves
>   pinch of saffron
>   2   tablespoons lime juice
>   additional salt to taste

Wash the fish, rub it with saffron, salt, and pepper, and set aside for 15 minutes to absorb the flavors. Then fry in vegetable oil until golden brown. In a separate skillet, heat the vegetable oil, and brown the onions and green chilies. Grind the cumin seeds, and add 1 cup of the milk, the garlic, rampa, curry leaves, and a pinch of saffron. Add this to the browned onions, and bring to a low boil. Add the remaining cup of milk, stirring continuously. Add salt and lime juice to taste. Add the fried fish slices, and simmer for about 5 minutes. *Serves 4.*

HOT FISH-BALL CURRY

    1 pound (2 cups) any meaty fish, boned and finely
      minced
 1½ teaspoons fresh garlic, chopped
    2 tablespoons onion, finely chopped
    1 tablespoon green chilies, chopped
    1 teaspoon fresh gingerroot, chopped
   10 curry leaves
      salt to taste

SIMMERING SAUCE

    1 tablespoon vegetable oil
    1 tablespoon onion, sliced
    1 cup coconut milk
    1 cup water
  ½ teaspoon curry powder
  ½ teaspoon ground turmeric
    1 tablespoon lemon juice
      Salt to taste

In a food processor or mixing bowl, combine the boned
and minced fish, garlic, onion, green chilies, ginger, and 5 of
the 10 curry leaves. Salt to taste. Form into about 15 two-inch
balls, making sure they are firm and tightly compressed. Set
them aside. In a medium-size skillet, heat the vegetable oil, and
brown the 5 remaining curry leaves and the onion. Then add
the coconut milk, water, curry powder, turmeric, and salt, and
bring to a boil. Spoon in the fish and spice balls, reducing the
liquid to simmer. Add the lemon juice, and cook for about 20
minutes or until the fish balls are cooked through. *Serves 4.*

HOT FISH SOUP

  6 cups water
 ½ pound (1 cup) fresh fish, such as tuna or halibut
 ½ large onion, finely chopped
  1 teaspoon crushed, dried red chilies
 ½ teaspoon black pepper
  1 cup leeks, chopped
  1 large potato, finely chopped
    salt to taste
  6 curry leaves
  1 tablespoon lemon juice
  5 green chilies, chopped

Pour the water into a large soup pot, and over low heat combine the fresh fish, onion, chilies, black pepper, leeks, and potato. Add salt to taste. Stir in the curry leaves. Mash the fish with a fork or with the fingers. Cook for about 30 minutes. Add the lemon juice about 5 minutes before the soup is done. If you'd like it even spicier, toss in 5 chopped green chilies. *Serves 4.*

HOT SMELT FRY

      2 pounds (4 cups) raw whole smelts
        dash of turmeric
        a sprinkle of salt
      ¼ cup lemon juice
 4 to 5 tablespoons vegetable oil for frying
      1 tablespoon crushed garlic
      1 tablespoon crushed, dried red chilies
      2 large onions, sliced
      3 large banana chilies
      1 large tomato, sliced
        Salt to taste

Wash the smelts and drain them well. Place the fish in a bowl, and sprinkle with turmeric, salt, and half the lemon juice. Coat well. Heat a few tablespoons of vegetable oil, and fry the smelts until golden brown and very crisp. Drain off the excess oil. Add the remaining spices and vegetables, and brown for about 6 minutes. If the fish is dry, add an additional tablespoon or two of oil. Add the remaining lemon juice and salt to taste. *Serves 4.*

MIRIS MALU FISH CURRY

   1 **pound (2 cups) any firm fresh fish, cut into one-inch chunks**
   2 **tablespoons lime juice**
   5 **pieces goraka**
   1 **teaspoon fresh gingerroot, finely chopped**
   1 **teaspoon ground black pepper**
1½ **teaspoons fresh garlic, minced**
   4 **teaspoons chili powder**
   2 **cups water, approximately**
     salt to taste

Place the fish in a mixing bowl. Sprinkle with the lime juice, making sure the fish is well coated and the juice is well rubbed into the fish. Boil the goraka in enough water to cover it until it is soft, and then mash it into a paste. In a medium-size saucepan, combine the remaining ingredients. Salt to taste. Add the marinated fish and cook over low heat until the fish is done (about 10 or 12 minutes) or until most of the gravy is very thick. This dish can be very tart and hot. *Serves 4.*

PICKLED FRIED FISH

    1 pound (2 cups) firm fish such as tuna or halibut,
         cut into bite-size pieces
    ½ teaspoon ground turmeric
         salt to taste (about 1 teaspoon)
3 to 4 tablespoons vegetable oil, approximately
    1 cup cider vinegar
    1 tablespoon tamarind paste or mashed tamarind
  1½ tablespoons ground coriander
    2 tablespoons sugar
    2 tablespoons chili powder
    2 cups water, approximately

Place the pieces of fish in a mixing bowl, and rub well with the turmeric and salt. Heat the vegetable oil and fry the fish until golden brown. In a separate saucepan, combine the remaining ingredients and water, and bring to a boil. Add the fried fish and cook another 5 minutes. Chill the pickled fried fish before serving with rice and curry. *Makes about one pound (about 4 side-dish servings).*

SALMON CURRY

  2 to 3 tablespoons vegetable oil
     ½ onion, sliced
   10 curry leaves
       pinch of lemongrass
    1 tablespoon fresh garlic, crushed
    3 one-inch pieces rampa
    ½ cinnamon stick
    1 teaspoon chili powder
    2 tablespoons curry powder (or 1 tablespoon each
       ground coriander and cumin)
    1 teaspoon ground turmeric
    1 cup water
    1 cup milk
   10 ounces (1¼ cups) fresh salmon, canned salmon,
       or mackerel

Heat the oil in a skillet, and brown the onions, curry leaves, lemongrass, garlic, and rampa. Lower the heat and add the cinnamon stick, chili powder, curry powder, and turmeric, and stir constantly for about 3 minutes. Then add the water and milk, and cook over low heat for another 3 minutes. Cut the salmon into one-inch pieces, and add to the skillet. Cook for approximately 10 to 15 minutes or until the fish is done. If it is precooked canned salmon, cook only until the mixture comes to a low boil. *Serves 4.*

SALMON DEVIL

  2 tablespoons ground mustard
  2 tablespoons crushed, dried red chilies
  ½ cup coconut milk or light cream
  8 curry leaves

1 tablespoon lemongrass, chopped
2 tablespoons ghee or vegetable oil
2 large onions, sliced
1 pound salmon filets or steak, cubed or whole

Combine the ground mustard, crushed red chilies, coconut milk, curry leaves, and lemongrass, and mix well. Heat the ghee or oil, and brown the sliced onions. Add the vegetable-and-spice mixture. Let it simmer for about 10 minutes. Then add the salmon, and simmer for another 10 minutes. Remove from heat. You may substitute chicken, beef, or lamb in this recipe, but you must cook it somewhat longer—at least half an hour. *Serves 4.*

TEMPERED DRY FISH

12 ounces (1½ cups) any dried, salted fish (codfish is good)
3 to 4 tablespoons vegetable oil
2 large onions, sliced
1 tablespoon fresh garlic, crushed
8 curry leaves
1 tablespoon crushed, dried red chilies
1 large tomato, sliced
1 tablespoon lemon juice
   salt to taste

Wash the fish and cut it into half-inch pieces. Heat the oil in a skillet. When it's very hot, add the fish and fry until golden-brown. Stir in the onion, garlic, curry leaves, red chilies, and tomato. Fry, stirring well, until the onions are golden-brown. Add the lemon juice, and salt to taste. Serve with rice. We call this dish a "rice puller"—because you end up eating more rice than you had planned. *Serves 4.*

LAMB

There are actually no lamb curries in Sri Lanka; sheep don't fare well in the heat. Goat meat (which the Sri Lankans call *mutton*) is very commonly used for meat curries, however. The good quality of lamb available to Western cooks will make a savory curry.

LAMB CUTLETS (CROQUETTES)

3 to 4 tablespoons vegetable oil
    1 pound (2 cups) ground lamb
    4 small potatoes, cooked and mashed
    4 green chilies
    1 teaspoon crushed, dried red chilies
   ½ teaspoon ground cumin
    1 sprig parsley, finely chopped
    1 teaspoon ground black pepper
       salt to taste (about 1½ teaspoons)
   ½ large onion, very finely chopped
3 or 4 beaten eggs
       bread crumbs
       vegetable oil for frying

Heat the oil in a saucepan, and add the ground lamb. Stir in the green and red chilies, cumin, parsley, black pepper, and add salt to taste. Cook until the meat is well browned, then add the onions. Remove from heat and cool. Then add the mashed potatoes and stir well. Divide into about 16 portions, forming balls or flat cutlets. Dip each ball into beaten egg, then into bread crumbs. Deep fry until golden brown. *Serves 4.*

PORK

BLACK PORK CURRY

    3 tablespoons curry powder
    1 teaspoon ground coriander
    ½ teaspoon ground turmeric
    2 tablespoons coarse black pepper
    3 tablespoons vegetable oil
    1 teaspoon fresh garlic, chopped
    ½ onion, chopped
    3 one-inch pieces rampa
    8 curry leaves
    4 pieces goraka, approximately
 1½ pounds (3 cups) pork, cubed
    ½ cup soy sauce
    5 cardamom pods, crushed
    2 cups water, optional

Dry-roast the curry powder, coriander, turmeric, and black pepper for about 5 minutes over low heat. When the mixture is dark-brown in color, add the vegetable oil. Sauté the garlic and onions in the hot oil, adding the rampa, curry leaves, and goraka. Continue to stir and add the pork, soy sauce, and cardamom. When the pork is thoroughly coated, you may add the water if you like more gravy. Cook over low heat until the pork is done (about 30 minutes). Serve with rice and one vegetable dish. *Serves 4.*

GORAKA PORK CURRY

    2 tablespoons curry powder
  10 curry leaves
3 to 4 tablespoons vegetable oil
    1 onion, sliced
    1 tablespoon garlic, crushed
 1½ pounds (3 cups) pork, cut into bite-size pieces
    5 pieces goraka, boiled and mashed into a paste
    5 cardamom pods
      salt to taste
    1 cup water

Dry-roast the curry powder and curry leaves over low heat until they are dark brown (about 15 or 20 minutes). Then add the oil, onion, and garlic, and fry for about 2 minutes. Stir in the pork, goraka paste, and cardamom pods, crushing the pods. Add salt to taste. Add the cup of water, and cook over low heat until the pork is cooked—about 30 minutes. *Serves 4.*

PORK CUTLETS (CROQUETTES)

        3 to 4 tablespoons vegetable oil
             1 pound (2 cups) ground pork
          1½ teaspoons salt
             4 green chilies
             1 sprig parsley, finely chopped
             1 teaspoon ground black pepper
           ½ large onion, finely chopped
             4 potatoes, cooked and mashed
        3 or 4 beaten eggs
                bread crumbs
                vegetable oil for deep frying

Heat the oil and brown the pork, adding the salt, chilies, parsley, and black pepper. Cook until the meat is well browned, and then add the onions. Remove from heat and cool. Add the mashed potatoes and stir well. Divide into about 16 portions, forming balls or flat cutlets. Dip each ball into beaten egg and then into bread crumbs. Deep-fry until golden brown. *Serves 4.*

SPICY SWEET-AND-SOUR PORK

             1 pound (2 cups) pork, cubed
             1 tablespoon flour
             1 beaten egg
        2 to 3 tablespoons vegetable oil
             2 ripe red tomatoes, sliced
             1 large onion, sliced
             1 teaspoon each fresh garlic and ginger, crushed
             2 tablespoons hot chili powder
           ¾ cup tomato sauce
             1 tablespoon sugar
             1 tablespoon cider vinegar
                salt and pepper to taste
                cornstarch (optional)

Fill a saucepan with sufficient water to cover the pork, and boil the meat until cooked through. Reserve the stock. Combine the flour and egg together in a medium-size mixing bowl, and dip each piece of pork in the mixture. Heat the vegetable oil in a skillet, and fry the pork until golden brown. To the pork stock add the sliced tomatoes, sliced onions, garlic, ginger, and chili powder, and simmer for about 5 minutes. Add the tomato sauce, sugar, and vinegar. Salt and pepper to taste. The mixture may be thickened with a bit of cornstarch. *Serves 4.*

SHELLFISH

BELL PEPPERS STUFFED WITH CRABMEAT

    12 medium bell peppers
3 to 4 tablespoons vegetable oil
    ½ onion, chopped
     1 teaspoon fresh garlic, minced
     2 cups crabmeat, chopped into bite-size segments
     1 teaspoon lemon juice
     1 teaspoon curry powder
     1 teaspoon chili powder
        salt to taste
     2 large potatoes, boiled and mashed

Wash peppers and split them in half. Remove the seeds. Heat the vegetable oil in a frying pan, and brown the onion and garlic. Then add the crabmeat morsels. Stir in the lemon juice, curry powder, and chili powder. Salt to taste. Cook over moderate heat about 5 minutes. Add the mashed potatoes. Cool the mixture and stuff into the pepper halves. You may top the peppers with a little grated cheese or chili sauce if you prefer. Place them in a baking dish, and bake at 350°F for about 20 minutes or until the peppers are slightly soft. You may also serve them without baking, if you like the peppers crunchy. *Serves 6.*

CRAB OMELETTE

8 large eggs
salt to taste
3 tablespoons vegetable oil or butter
1 cup crabmeat, chopped or crushed into small pieces
1 teaspoon crushed, dried red chilies
2 tablespoons chopped or shredded carrots
2 tablespoons cabbage, well chopped
2 tablespoons leeks, chopped
2 tablespoons onion, finely chopped
2 tablespoons fresh mushrooms, sliced
2 tablespoons fresh or frozen spinach, chopped
½ teaspoon curry powder

Beat the eggs in a large mixing bowl, and add salt to taste. Stir in the crabmeat, chilies, vegetables, and curry powder. Set aside. Heat the vegetable oil or butter in a medium-size skillet (you may use an omelette pan). Pour in ¼ to ½ cup of the egg and crabmeat-vegetable mixture, and cook a minute or two. Then flip it over and continue to cook until done to desired dryness. Serve whole or cut into strips. Repeat procedure to make 4 omlettes. *Serves 4.*

CURRIED LOBSTER

   2 tablespoons vegetable oil
   ½ onion, sliced
   1½ teaspoons garlic, minced
   1½ teaspoons freshly grated gingerroot
   6 to 8 curry leaves
   1 one-inch piece lemongrass (fresh is best)
   3 whole 1-pound lobsters, cut into chunks, shells and all
   2 tablespoons curry powder (or 1 tablespoon each cumin and coriander)
   1 tablespoon chili powder
     salt to taste
   2 cups coconut milk
   2 tablespoons lemon juice

Heat the oil in a pan, and brown the onion, garlic, ginger, curry leaves, and lemongrass. Add the lobster chunks and stir continuously over medium heat. Add the curry powder and chili powder. Make sure the powder is well distributed on each piece of lobster. Add salt to taste. Cook over medium to low heat for about 5 minutes. Add the coconut milk while stirring, and add more water if you need more sauce. Add the lemon juice, and reduce heat. Cook for 5 minutes. Serve over rice. *Serves 4.*

CURRIED SQUID

   2 pounds squid, fresh is best, but good frozen and thawed squid are available
   2 tablespoons vegetable oil
   ½ onion, sliced
   3 green chilies, sliced
   1 tablespoon fresh garlic, minced
   1 tablespoon fresh gingerroot, minced

  10 curry leaves
   1 three-inch piece lemongrass, chopped
   1 one-inch piece cinnamon stick
   4 cardamom seeds, crushed
1½ tablespoons curry powder
   1 tablespoon chili powder
      salt to taste
   2 cups coconut milk or light cream
   1 cup water, approximately
   1 tablespoon lemon juice

Wash the squid and, if it is fresh, clean it by removing the ink sack and the sharp, transparent inner membranes called *pen*, or *chitin* (backbone). Slice the squid into rings. Heat the oil in a skillet, and brown the onion, chilies, garlic, ginger, curry leaves, lemongrass, cinnamon, and cardamom. Add the squid, and keep stirring as you add the curry powder and chili powder. Continue to stir, and add salt to taste. Cook about 5 minutes. Add the coconut milk and about a cup of water if you need more gravy. Add the lemon juice, and simmer a few more minutes. Serve with rice and a vegetable dish or two. *Serves 4.*

DEVILED HOT AND SPICY LOBSTER

3 to 4 tablespoons vegetable oil
    1 large onion, sliced
    1 teaspoon fresh garlic, minced
    1 teaspoon ginger, freshly grated
    2 whole 1-pound lobsters, shells and all, chopped into segments
   10 curry leaves
    1 heaping teaspoon curry powder
    5 banana chilies, sliced
    1 tablespoon crushed, dried red chilies
    1 cup kale, chopped
    2 tablespoons lemon juice

Heat the oil in a large frying pan. Add the onion, garlic, ginger, and the lobster segments. Add the curry leaves, and brown lightly. Stir in the curry powder, banana chilies, and crushed red chilies. Then add the kale and lemon juice. Continue to stir, and cook over low heat until the lobster is done —usually 12 minutes or less. If you find it's too dry, add ½ cup water. Serve over rice. *Serves 4. Note*: If you'd prefer this dish milder, leave out the crushed red chilies.

FIREWORKS PRAWNS

3 large ripe tomatoes, crushed
1 teaspoon cider vinegar
  a dash of salt
1 tablespoon chili powder
3 tablespoons bacon fat
1 large onion, sliced
1 pound (2 cups) large prawns, deveined
2 tablespoons cornstarch
2 tablespoons parsley, chopped
4 green chilies, chopped
  salt and pepper to taste

In a medium-size pot, combine the crushed tomato, vinegar, salt, and chili powder. Cook for about 15 minutes and set aside. In a skillet, heat the bacon fat and brown the onions. Add the prawns and cornstarch, and cook, stirring slowly, until the prawns are golden brown. Add in the tomato mixture, parsley, and green chilies. Salt and pepper to taste. Cook for a few more minutes. This is a real "rice puller"—it makes you want to eat more and more rice! *Serves 4.*

HOT PICKLED PRAWNS

        1 teaspoon brown mustard seeds
        3 tablespoons cider vinegar
        1 teaspoon fresh garlic, minced
        1 teaspoon fresh ginger, chopped
        1 tablespoon sugar
          salt to taste
        2 tablespoons vegetable oil
       20 medium to large prawns, cleaned
       ½ cup seedless dates
        1 onion, sliced
        3 banana chilies, sliced
        1 tablespoon chili powder
   3 to 6 pieces dried mango (optional)

In a food processor or electric blender, grind together the mustard seed, vinegar, garlic, and ginger. Add more vinegar if the mixture is too thick. Add the sugar, and salt to taste. Heat the vegetable oil in a skillet, and cook the prawns until they are golden brown. Stir in the dates, onions, banana chilies, chili powder, and dried mango, and cook for 10 minutes. This dish keeps well if refrigerated and may also be served cold. *Serves 4.*

HOT PRAWN STEW

Stews are typical of the British influence in Sri Lanka in the last century and a half. My father used to make this stew and his second specialty, a fish-head stew, by cooking them all day in a huge pot over a simple brick-framed fire outdoors in the garden. Serve this one with rice on the side, of course.

   6 to 8 cups water
        4 potatoes, cut into bite-size pieces
        1 carrot, cut into bite-size pieces
        1 large onion, sliced
        3 whole cloves

1 teaspoon ground mustard
1 teaspoon sugar
6 banana chilies, sliced
1½ tablespoons worcestershire sauce
1 pound (2 cups) large prawns, shells on or off
   salt to taste

Bring the water to a boil in a kettle, and add the potatoes, carrot, and onion. Wait 5 minutes, and then add the other ingredients except the prawns. When the vegetables are tender, add the prawns and add salt to taste. Cook until the prawns are plump and done (about 6 minutes). You may add a cup of coconut milk if you prefer a thicker gravy. *Serves 4. Note*: You may use this recipe for beef stew as well—just cook it a bit longer, until the beef is tender.

LARGE PRAWN BADUM*

½ cup vegetable oil
10 curry leaves
1 cup sliced onion
1 teaspoon fresh gingerroot, crushed
1 teaspoon fresh garlic, minced
½ teaspoon ground turmeric
1 tablespoon crushed, dried red chilies
3 cardamom pods, crushed
1 one-inch piece of stick cinnamon
1 tablespoon lime juice
1½ pounds (3 cups) large prawns, deveined (shells on
   or off)
   salt to taste

Heat the oil in a skillet, and brown the curry leaves and onion. Add the ginger, garlic, turmeric, red chilies, cardamom,

Badum is a Sinhalese style of cooking; frying.

and cinnamon. Stir in the lime juice and the prawns, and cook until the prawns are firm. Add salt to taste. This dish will keep well if refrigerated for a few days. *Serves 4.*

PRAWNS AND PINEAPPLE

½ **cup whiskey**
1 **tablespoon soy sauce**
1 **teaspoon salt**
½ **teaspoon ground black pepper**
15 **large prawns, deveined**
4 **tablespoons vegetable oil**
1 **teaspoon chili powder**
1 **cup chopped pineapple, fresh or canned**
¼ **cup onion, chopped**
½ **cup parsley, chopped**

In a mixing bowl, combine the whiskey, soy sauce, salt, pepper, and prawns. Allow to sit for about 20 minutes. Heat the vegetable oil in a skillet. Add the prawns, retaining the whiskey sauce for later. Stir-fry for about 5 minutes. Stir in chili powder, pineapple, onion, and the whiskey sauce. Cook about 15 minutes. Serve over rice or Chinese noodles garnished with chopped parsley. *Serves 4. Note:* You may make this dish with pork instead of prawns, but be sure to cook it longer—at least a total of 30 minutes.

PRAWN CURRY

   2 pounds (4 cups) prawns (large shrimp in the shell)
   1 tablespoon chili powder (use paprika if you prefer a milder dish that still has color)
   3 cloves fresh garlic, minced
   2 one-inch pieces gingerroot, crushed
   1 one-inch piece rampa
   1 one-inch piece lemongrass
 10 curry leaves
      salt to taste
      juice of 1 lemon or lime
   2 tablespoons vegetable oil
   2 cups coconut milk or light cream

If you prefer your prawns shelled, clean them by snapping off the tails, skinning off the shells, and picking out the dark vein along their backs. Heat a frying pan and dry-roast the prawns, adding the chili powder, garlic, ginger, rampa, lemongrass, and curry leaves. Salt to taste. Mix well with the lime or lemon juice, and cook over medium heat until the liquids evaporate. Then add the vegetable oil, and fry the prawns until golden brown. Add the milk and simmer over low heat for about 10 minutes. *Serves 4.*

PRAWN SOUP

   3 tablespoons vegetable oil or butter
   5 curry leaves
   1 cup green onions, chopped
   1 teaspoon fresh garlic, minced
 ½ teaspoon chili powder
   5 cups water
 ½ cup dhal (lentils)
      a pinch of black pepper
      salt to taste

15 medium-size prawns, cleaned and cut into bite-size pieces
1 cup fresh spinach, finely chopped

Heat the butter in a soup pot, and brown the curry leaves and the green onions. Add the garlic and chili powder, and brown for another minute. Stir in the water, dhal, and pepper, and salt to taste. Cook over low heat for approximately 15 minutes or until the dhal is soft. Finally, add the prawns, and cook until they are firm (about 5 minutes). Just before serving, top with the finely chopped spinach. *Serves 4.*

SHRIMP NOODLES

2 to 3 tablespoons vegetable oil
½ onion, chopped
1 teaspoon fresh garlic, minced
½ pound (1 cup) shrimp, cut into bite-size pieces
1 teaspoon curry powder
1 tablespoon chili powder
8 curry leaves
1 cup mushrooms, chopped
2 cups fresh spinach, kale, broccoli, or other vegetable, chopped
1 cup coconut milk or light cream
2 servings (about 2 cups uncooked) Chinese noodles, precooked (or egg noodles cooked and drained)
salt to taste

Heat the oil in a pan, and brown the onions and garlic. Add the shrimp, and sauté for about 3 minutes. Stir in the curry powder, chili powder, curry leaves, mushrooms, and whatever additional vegetables you prefer. Add the coconut milk, and cook for about 2 minutes. Then add the noodles. Combine and cook for 1 minute, and salt to taste. You may add more shrimp and vegetables and make this a main dish, otherwise it's a good side dish. *Serves 2.*

SMALL DRIED SHRIMP (KOONI MALLUNG)

2 to 3 cups dried shrimp
   1 teaspoon saffron (or turmeric)
   1 large onion, chopped
   3 green chilies, chopped
   1 large tomato, chopped
   6 curry leaves
     salt to taste
   3 tablespoons vegetable oil
  ½ cup fresh coconut, grated (you may substitute unsweetened dessicated coconut)

Kooni are very tiny dried shrimp. (Wash them before using.) If they are unavailable, use the smallest dried shrimp available (do not wash these) and crush by hand or in a food processor. Place the shrimp in a pan with the saffron, onion, green chilies, tomato, and curry leaves. Salt to taste, and dry-roast the mixture for a few minutes until the moisture evaporates. Add the vegetable oil, and stir-fry the mixture for a few minutes. Add the coconut. Continue to cook and stir for 5 minutes. If you like the dish "hotter," add about 6 to 8 more hot green chilies. *Serves 4.*

STUFFED CURRIED SQUID

2 pounds fresh squid, cleaned

STUFFING

2 to 3 tablespoons vegetable oil, or slightly more as
      needed
1 onion, chopped
2 potatoes, peeled and finely chopped
8 large shrimp, peeled and chopped
  salt and pepper to taste
  lemon juice

CURRY SAUCE

2 to 3 tablespoons vegetable oil
1 teaspoon fresh gingerroot, minced
1 teaspoon fresh garlic, chopped
1 tablespoon chili powder
1 tablespoon curry powder
½ teaspoon turmeric
10 curry leaves
4 cardamom pods, crushed
1 three-inch piece lemongrass
2 cups coconut milk or light cream

Separate the tentacle sections from the torso sections of the
cleaned squid, wash both, and set aside. Heat about 1 tablespoon
of the vegetable oil in a skillet, and brown half the chopped
onions. Add the potatoes and brown. Then add the shrimp, and
cook for about 3 minutes. Salt and pepper the mixture to taste,
and set aside to cool. When cool, add a dash of lemon juice.

Work a small amount of stuffing into each squid torso with
the fingers or a small spoon. Close the squid with a toothpick
so the stuffing does not fall out.

To make the curry sauce: heat the vegetable oil in a pan and brown the remaining onions, adding the garlic and ginger. Add chili powder, curry powder, turmeric, curry leaves, cardamom, and lemongrass, and continue to stir over medium heat for about 5 more minutes. Then add the coconut milk and reduce the heat. Slip the stuffed squid into the sauce, and cook gently for about 20 minutes or until the squid is done, continually coating the squid with the sauce. Serve with rice and a vegetable dish. *Serves 4.*

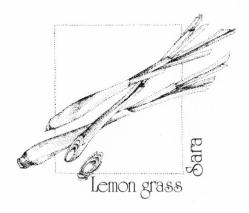

Lemon grass   Sara

TEMPERED PRAWNS

    1 pound (2 cups) medium to large prawns in their
       shells
    3 tablespoons vegetable oil
   10 curry leaves
    1 three-inch piece rampa
   ½ large onion, chopped
    1 half-inch piece cinnamon stick
    3 teaspoons chili powder
   ½ teaspoon turmeric
  1½ teaspoons fresh garlic, chopped
   ½ teaspoon salt
   ½ teaspoon ground coriander

Devein and wash the prawns, leaving the tails and shells on. Heat the oil in a pan, and add the curry leaves, rampa, onion, cinnamon. Toss until the onions are slightly brown. Add the prawns and the rest of the ingredients. Cook over medium heat and keep tossing till the prawns are firm (about 6 minutes). Serve with rice. *Serves 4.*

TEMPERED SQUID

2	pounds (4 cups) fresh squid, cleaned
3 to 4	tablespoons vegetable oil
1	onion, sliced
½	tablespoon lemongrass, crushed
10	curry leaves
	salt to taste
1	teaspoon crushed, dried red chilies
1	teaspoon curry powder
1	teaspoon fresh garlic, finely chopped
½	teaspoon fresh gingerroot, finely chopped
1	cup fresh mushrooms, sliced
1	cup coconut milk or light cream
1	teaspoon lemon juice

Wash the squid, removing the ink sack and membrane. Slice the squid into rings about a half-inch thick. Heat the vegetable oil in a skillet, and add the onion, lemongrass, and curry leaves. Fry for about 2 minutes. Then slide in the squid, and stir and toss for about 2 minutes. Add salt to taste. Then stir in the red chilies, curry powder, garlic, ginger, and mushrooms, and toss for another 3 minutes. Add the coconut milk, and bring it to a boil. Before removing from stove, add the lemon juice and a little water if you prefer more gravy. Serve over rice. *Serves 4.*

VEGETARIAN DISHES

BEET CURRY

   1 pound (2 cups) fresh, raw beets, approximately
   3 tablespoons vegetable oil
   8 curry leaves
   3 green chilies, chopped
  ½ onion, chopped
   1 teaspoon sugar
   2 teaspoons chili powder
   1 teaspoon ground coriander
   2 teaspoons cider vinegar
   2 teaspoons salt
 1½ cups coconut milk, regular milk, or light cream

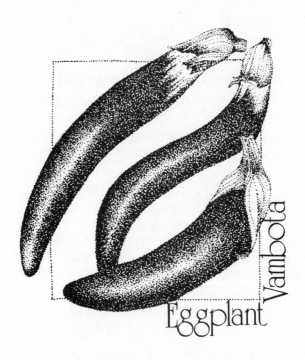

Eggplant Vambota

Peel and wash the beets; cut them into very thin strips. Heat oil in a pan and add the curry leaves, green chilies, onion, sugar, chili powder, coriander, and vinegar. Fry for about 5 minutes or until the onions are light brown. Add the beets and salt. Stir constantly for a few minutes over low heat. Add the milk and simmer until the beets are tender. This is a great side dish. Radishes, baby carrots, and regular carrots may also be cooked this way. *Serves 4.*

BRINJAL CURRY (EGGPLANT CURRY)

1	pound (2 cups) eggplant
¼	teaspoon ground turmeric
1½	teaspoons salt
	vegetable oil for deep frying, about 2 cups
2	green chilies
2	small onions, chopped
2	teaspoons ground coriander
1	teaspoon ground cumin
10	curry leaves
1	two-inch piece of stick cinnamon
1	cup milk
1½	teaspoons salt
3	cloves garlic, chopped
1½	teaspoons ground mustard
2	teaspoons sugar
1	two-inch piece rampa (optional)

Slice the eggplant into thin, two-inch-long pieces. Sprinkle it with turmeric and salt, and fry it in hot vegetable oil until golden brown. Combine the remaining ingredients in a saucepan with the milk. Bring the mixture to a boil, add the fried eggplant, and simmer until the juices are thick. *Serves 4.*

BROCCOLI MALLUNG

3 to 4 tablespoons vegetable oil or butter
½ onion, chopped
½ teaspoon fresh garlic, crushed
¼ cup crushed dried shrimp (optional)
2 teaspoons crushed, dried red chilies
½ teaspoon turmeric
½ teaspoon ground cumin
½ cup unsweetened coconut, dried or fresh
2 large stalks of broccoli chopped fine, stems and all
salt to taste

Heat the oil in a large skillet or frying pan. Brown the onion, garlic, and dried shrimp. Add the red dried chilies, turmeric, and cumin, and brown for a minute. Then stir in the coconut, and brown for another minute. Add the chopped broccoli and salt to taste. Cook uncovered for about 5 minutes. *Serves 4.*

CABBAGE MALLUNG

1 cup red or white cabbage, thinly sliced or shredded
3 to 4 tablespoons vegetable oil
½ teaspoon mustard seeds
½ onion, chopped
1 teaspoon fresh garlic, minced
1 tablespoon crushed, dried red chilies
½ cup desiccated coconut
¼ teaspoon turmeric
2 teaspoons ground cumin
salt to taste

Slice cabbage into very thin strips. Heat the oil in a frying pan, add the mustard seeds, and cover. When the seeds start to pop, add the onion, garlic, red pepper, and coconut and brown for about 5 minutes. Then add the turmeric and cumin and toss for another 2 minutes. Add the thinly sliced cabbage, salt to taste, and cook covered for about 2 minutes. Remove from heat. This dish is best when the cabbage is slightly crisp or half raw. It is traditionally served with rice and a meat curry. *Serves 2.*

CABBAGE THALDALA*

          3 to 4 tablespoons vegetable oil or margarine
             ½ onion, sliced
             1 tablespoon fresh garlic, minced
             6 curry leaves (optional)
             4 green chilies
             1 teaspoon crushed, dried red chilies
             ½ teaspoon turmeric
             1 tablespoon curry powder or cumin
             1 medium cabbage, thinly sliced
                salt to taste

Using a large frying pan, heat the oil and brown the onions. Then add the garlic, curry leaves, chopped green chilies, and red chilies. Stir in the turmeric and curry powder. Cook for about 3 minutes, then add cabbage. Salt to taste. Cook an additional 5 or 6 minutes, stirring constantly. You may fry this dish until the cabbage is tender or stop when it is faintly crunchy, depending on your taste. *Serves 4.*

Thaldala is the Sinhalese word for "cooking with oil."

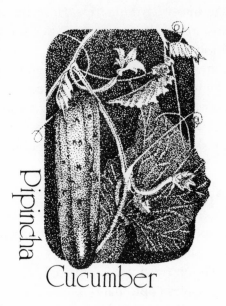

Pipincha
Cucumber

CUCUMBER-TOMATO-CHILI SALAD

- 1 cup (about 2 medium-size) cucumbers, peeled and sliced
- 3 medium tomatoes, sliced
- 1 large onion, sliced
- 6 green chilies, sliced
- ¼ cup fresh parsley, finely chopped
- ¼ cup celery, chopped
- ¼ cup Heather's mustard sauce (see recipe under Sambols), or Ingelhoffer's mustard, or any whole-grain mustard
- 2 teaspoons sugar
- salt

Combine the cucumbers, tomatoes, onion, green chilies, parsley, and celery in a bowl. Stir in mustard sauce and sugar, and salt to taste. *Serves 4.*

CURRIED CASHEWS

3	cups unsalted, raw cashew nuts
3 to 4	tablespoons vegetable oil
½	onion, chopped
2	teaspoons ground coriander
1	teaspoon ground cumin
1	teaspoon fenugreek powder
3	teaspoons chili powder
1	one-inch cinnamon stick
½	teaspoon turmeric
10	curry leaves
2	whole cloves
2	cardamom pods, crushed
1½	teaspoons salt
1	cup coconut milk or light cream

Boil the raw cashews in water until they are tender, but not soft—about 6 minutes. Heat the oil in a skillet, and when it is very hot, add all ingredients except the cashews, salt, and coconut milk. Brown slightly. Add the cashews and salt, and cook about 10 minutes. Add the milk, bring to a boil, and serve. If you like a yellow curry that is less spicy, leave out the chili powder. *Serves 4 to 6.*

CURRIED PUMPKIN OR SQUASH

        3 cups pumpkin or firm squash
   3 to 4 tablespoons vegetable oil
        1 tablespoon mustard seed
       ½ onion, chopped
        1 tablespoon fresh garlic, minced
       ½ cup desiccated coconut
        2 cups water
        2 teaspoons crushed, dried red chilies
       ½ teaspoon ground turmeric
          about 10 curry leaves
      1½ cups coconut milk or light cream
          salt to taste

Wash the pumpkin and remove the seeds. Cut into two-inch
pieces. Heat the oil in a saucepan, and add the mustard seeds.
As they start to pop, add the chopped onion, garlic, and coconut,
and brown. Then add the remaining ingredients, except for salt
and pumpkin. Mix well and cook for about 4 minutes. Add the
pumpkin and salt together with the water, and cook until the
pumpkin is soft. You may thicken the gravy by adding more
coconut milk. *Serves 6 to 8.*

CURRIED TOMATOES

   3 to 4 tablespoons vegetable oil
        3 green chilies, coarsely chopped
       ½ onion, chopped
        2 teaspoons garlic, minced
        2 teaspoons fresh gingerroot, grated
        2 tablespoons crushed dried shrimp
        1 tablespoon ground cumin
        2 teaspoons ground coriander
        1 tablespoon chili powder
       10 curry leaves

2 cups green tomatoes, sliced
salt to taste

Heat the oil and brown the green chilies, onion, garlic, ginger, and dried shrimp. Then add the cumin, coriander, chili powder, and curry leaves, and fry for about 2 minutes. Add the tomatoes, mix well, and cook over very low heat. Salt to taste, and cook until the tomatoes are soft. If you like more sauce, add more water. *Serves 4.*

DEVILED POTATOES

6 medium potatoes
3 to 4 tablespoons vegetable oil
2 large onions, sliced
4 banana chilies, sliced
salt to taste
1 tablespoon crushed, dried red chilies
10 curry leaves
½ cinnamon stick
1 teaspoon ground turmeric

Boil the potatoes until cooked but firm, and set aside. When cool, cut into one-inch cubes. Heat the vegetable oil in a large skillet, and add the onions and chilies. Add the cubed potatoes. Salt to taste. Add the remaining ingredients, and stir until the potatoes are well-coated with spices. Then cook over low heat until the potatoes are thoroughly done. *Serves 4.*

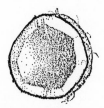  

EGGPLANT AND CHILI PICKLE

  4 medium eggplants
    pinch of saffron or turmeric
    a dash of salt
    vegetable oil for frying, as needed
 20 green chilies, sliced or chopped
  1 tablespoon crushed, dried red chilies
  1 tablespoon mustard seeds, crushed
  2 tablespoons ground coriander
  1 tablespoon ground cumin
  1 tablespoon each crushed fresh garlic and gingerroot
 ½ cup cider vinegar
 10 curry leaves
  1 two-inch piece cinnamon stick
  1 two-inch piece rampa
  1 two-inch piece lemongrass
    salt to taste

Cut the eggplant in thin pieces lengthwise. Rub each piece with saffron and salt, and fry in the hot vegetable oil until the eggplant is brown. In a separate skillet, sauté the green chilies for about 2 minutes. Combine the dried red chilies, mustard seeds, coriander, cumin, garlic, ginger, and vinegar. Add the fried eggplant, curry leaves, cinnamon, rampa, and lemongrass, and mix well. Salt to taste. *Note*: Sometimes mixing gently with your fingers is best, since a spoon might crush the eggplant. This dish keeps well for a long time in the refrigerator if it is tightly bottled. *Makes about three 8-ounce jars.*

FRIED EGGPLANT SALAD

  3 medium-size eggplants, sliced in thin rounds
    a dash of salt
  1 teaspoon ground turmeric
    vegetable oil for frying, as needed

1 large onion, sliced in thin rings
3 green chilies, thinly sliced
1 large tomato, thinly sliced
1½ teaspoons cider vinegar

Sprinkle the eggplant slices with the salt and turmeric, and fry until golden brown. Allow the slices to cool and arrange them flat on a platter. Combine the remaining ingredients and top each eggplant slice with the mixture. *Serves 4.*

GREEN BEAN MALLUNG

1 cup green beans, preferably the long, thin Chinese variety
4 green chilies
½ onion
3 cloves of garlic
2 tablespoons butter
2 tablespoons crushed dried shrimp (vegetarians may omit)
½ cup grated coconut
½ teaspoon ground turmeric
1 teaspoon ground coriander or curry powder
2 teaspoons salt

Wash the beans and slice them very thin lengthwise. Slice or chop the green chilies, onion, and garlic. Melt the butter in a saucepan, and brown the onions, garlic, and chilies with the dried shrimp. Add the beans, and simmer until tender. Add the coconut and the rest of the ingredients, and cook over low heat for about 10 minutes, stirring constantly, until the beans are done to your preferred degree of tenderness. *Serves 2.*

Garlic Sudhu lunu

KALE MALLUNG

> 1 or 2 bunches kale
> ½ large onion, chopped
> 1 tablespoon fresh garlic, chopped (about 3 large cloves)
> 3 to 4 tablespoons vegetable oil
> 1 tablespoon crushed, dried red chilies
> 1 teaspoon salt
> ½ cup grated fresh or desiccated coconut
> ½ teaspoon ground turmeric
> ¼ cup crushed dried shrimp

Wash the kale, and chop very fine. Heat the oil in a large skillet, and brown all ingredients except the kale (about 5 minutes). Add the kale and toss for about 5 minutes longer. Add about 2 tablespoons water to prevent the kale from burning. Serve as a side dish. *Serves 4.*

MANGO CURRY

    2 cups green mango, sliced
    3 teaspoons chili powder
    1 one-inch piece cinnamon stick
    ½ teaspoon ground cumin
    2 tablespoons cider vinegar
    1 tablespoon fresh garlic, chopped
    1 tablespoon fresh gingerroot, chopped
    2 tablespoons ground mustard
    2 teaspoons ground coriander
    2 teaspoons salt
    ½ cup coconut milk, regular milk, or light cream
    ½ cup water

Combine all ingredients in a large pot, add the water, and simmer on low heat until the mango is tender. *Serves 4.*

OKRA SALAD (LADIES' FINGERS SALAD)

    10 okra, cut in half lengthwise
     1 large onion, sliced
     3 green chilies, sliced
     1 teaspoon cider vinegar
     ½ teaspoon black pepper
     ½ teaspoon garlic powder
       salt to taste

Blanch the okra in enough hot, salted water to cover the okra. (Bring a pot of lightly salted water to a boil and drop in the okra. Cook for 30 to 40 seconds—do not overcook.) Remove from pot and place in a serving dish. Combine the onion, green chilies, vinegar, black pepper, and garlic powder, and pour over the okra. Salt to taste, and chill before serving. *Serves 4.*

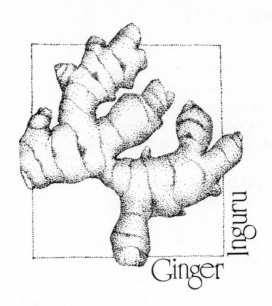

Ginger Inguru

PUMPKIN CURRY

> 2 cups pumpkin, cut into two-inch cubes, with skin
>   on and seeds removed
> 1 tablespoon chili powder or paprika
> 1 tablespoon curry powder
> 2 one-inch slices gingerroot, chopped
> 3 cloves fresh garlic, minced
> 1 one-inch piece lemongrass (or rampa)
> 2 cups coconut milk, light cream, or regular milk
>   salt to taste
> 2 tablespoons vegetable oil
> 1 teaspoon mustard seed
> 1 onion, sliced
> 3 or 4 dried crushed red chilies
> 10 curry leaves

Place the cubed pumpkin in a mixing bowl. Combine with
the chili powder, curry powder, ginger, garlic, lemongrass, and

coconut milk. Salt to taste and set aside. Heat the vegetable oil in a skillet and add the mustard seed. Brown the onion and whole chilies, breaking the latter up with a spoon. Add the curry leaves. When the onions are golden, add the pumpkin mixture, and cook for 15 minutes over medium heat or until the pumpkin is soft. *Serves 4.*

RED-HOT PUMPKIN CURRY

     3 cups pumpkin, cut into two-inch cubes, with skin on and seeds removed
3 to 4 tablespoons vegetable oil
     2 tablespoons chili powder
     1 one-inch piece cinnamon stick
     2 cardamom pods, crushed
     2 whole cloves
     2 tablespoons ground coriander
     2 tablespoons ground cumin
     2 teaspoons fresh garlic, chopped
     2 teaspoons fresh gingerroot, grated
     4 green chilies, sliced
  10 curry leaves
      salt to taste (about 2 teaspoons)
     2 cups water
     1 cup coconut milk or light cream

Wash the pumpkin, remove the seeds, and cut into two-inch pieces. Heat the oil in a skillet. Add the chili powder and fry for about 1 minute or less, being careful not to burn it. Add the remaining spices and vegetables and the pumpkin pieces. Toss the mixture gently until the pumpkin is coated with the spices. Salt to taste. Add the water and milk, and simmer until the pumpkin is tender (about 10 minutes). *Serves 4.*

VEGETABLE CURRY

          3 green chilies, sliced
        ½ onion, chopped
        ½ teaspoon ground turmeric
        ½ cinnamon stick
        ½ teaspoon fresh garlic, minced
        ½ teaspoon fresh gingerroot, chopped
          3 one-inch pieces lemongrass
          4 pieces rampa (optional)
        10 curry leaves
          salt to taste
          3 cups coconut milk (canned coconut milk or 2%
            milk are good substitutes)
          2 cups water
    3 to 4 cups sliced vegetables (cabbage, string beans,
            okra, potatoes, zucchini, or tomato)

In a soup pot, combine the chilies, onion, turmeric, cinnamon stick, garlic, ginger, lemongrass, rampa, and curry leaves. Add 1 cup of the coconut milk and the water, salt to taste, and gently simmer for about 8 to 10 minutes. Add the sliced vegetables, and cook until they are tender. Add the remaining 2 cups of coconut milk, and simmer another 5 minutes. This may be served with white rice and one meat dish. *Serves 4.*

VEGETABLE CUTLETS (CROQUETTES)

        ½ cup carrots, chopped
        ½ cup potatoes, chopped
        ¾ cup spinach, chopped
        ¼ cup uncooked dhal (lentils)
    3 to 4 tablespoons vegetable oil
        ¾ cup onions, chopped
          2 teaspoons fresh garlic, minced
          4 green chilies, finely chopped

1½ teaspoons salt
10 curry leaves
 1 tablespoon ground black pepper
½ teaspoon ground cumin
   bread crumbs, about 1 cup
 3 eggs, beaten
 2 cups vegetable oil approximately, for deep frying

Combine the chopped carrots, potatoes and spinach with the dhal in a small soup pot. Add water sufficient to cover, and boil briefly until vegetables and dhal are slightly tender. Drain off excess water. Heat the oil in a pan, and fry the onion, garlic, and green chilies until golden brown. Add the salt, curry leaves, black pepper, and cumin. Continue stirring over medium heat until the mixture is somewhat dry. Allow it to cool, then mash the mixture with the vegetables and dhal by hand or electric mixer. Form the cutlet "dough" into about 16 patties. If the dough is too wet, add a small amount of bread crumbs until it is dry enough to form patties. Dip each patty into beaten egg, roll in bread crumbs, and fry in hot oil until light brown. *Makes 8 to 16 cutlets.*

WHITE CUCUMBER CURRY

 2 cups cucumbers, peeled and cut into bite-sized
   pieces
 4 green chilies, sliced
½ onion, chopped
10 curry leaves
   pinch of ground turmeric
½ teaspoon ground cumin
1½ cups milk
 1 teaspoon ground mustard

Combine the cucumbers with the next five ingredients. Add the milk and simmer over low heat for about 6 minutes. Add the mustard, bring to a boil, and then reduce the heat. Cook another 5 minutes. White curry is best served with white rice, a meat curry, and one hot sambol. For a classic rice-and-curry meal. *Serves 4.*

WHITE POTATO CURRY

      6 medium-size potatoes, skin on
3 to 4 tablespoons vegetable oil
    ½ onion, chopped
      1 teaspoon chopped garlic
      4 curry leaves
    ½ cinnamon stick
      1 teaspoon crushed, dried red chilies
    ½ teaspoon turmeric
      1 teaspoon ground cumin
      1 large tomato, cut in medium-size chunks
      2 cups milk, either coconut or regular
      1 cup water

Boil the potatoes skin and all. Cool. Cut into bite-size bits, and set aside. Heat the oil in a skillet and brown the onion and garlic. Add the curry leaves, cinnamon stick, red chilies, turmeric, cumin, and tomato. Fry for a few minutes, stirring well to prevent burning. Add the milk and the water, and bring to a boil. Add the potatoes and cook for about 10 minutes over medium-low heat. *Serves 4 to 6.*

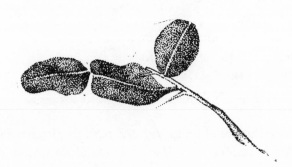

CHAPTER 10

SIDE DISHES
Grains, Noodles, and Lampries

Like many Third World countries where cuisine is based on grains, Sri Lanka has an abundance of varieties of rice that would shame a Western market. There is pearl rice, basmati rice (an Indian import), dark-red rice (especially filling and aromatic), pink rice, samba rice, brown rice, and dozens of white rice species. Sri Lankans consume so much rice that many buy their rice in big gunny sacks, often from relatives who own rice farms or are in some way involved in the rice business.

Sri Lankans eat leftover rice for breakfast with any leftover curry or a sambol. The easiest way is to heat a couple of tea-spoons of margarine or butter and add about half a teaspoon of mustard seeds and a few whole dried red peppers. When the mustard seeds start to pop, you add half a sliced onion and brown it. Then you add the leftover rice, and stir-fry for a few minutes.

Rice is also an integral part of the April New Year celebration for Sri Lankan people of many faiths. On a date established by the lunar calendar, Sri Lankans fast most of the day and dress

133

in specific colors designated as fortunate by the local astrologers. At the auspicious time, families gather to light the cooking fire—an honor that falls to someone considered especially prosperous.

Then the milk rice is cooked. For good luck, the Sinhalese allow the milk rice to boil over the pot—a symbol of abundance. It's especially auspicious if the pot overflows equally on all sides, because it represents good fortune from all directions. Tamils cook this dish until the milk puffs up and only then lift it off the fire. For the Tamils, boiling over is considered bad luck, because it wastes food. Some Sinhalese families pour the blend into tiny, new clay pots and sprinkle it around the home; Tamils, on the other hand, won't step on milk, since it would be a dishonor to the sacred Hindu animal, the cow. (Cows, by the way, are bathed as part of the New Year celebration; their necks are adorned with garlands of garlic; and the *potu*, a spot of saffron, is placed on their foreheads.)

The New Year is the only time Sri Lankans exchange gifts with relatives and friends. They walk or ride from house to house and bring trays of sweets; in return they are given sweets and tobacco wrapped in betel nut leaves. This is also the day when parents are venerated—children kneel and touch their parents' feet and offer a prayer of thanksgiving to them.

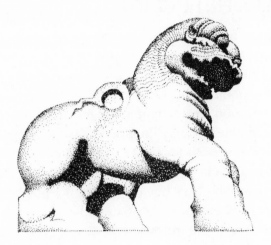

BEST NOODLE DISH, *Nasigoreng Style*

4 to 5 ounces butter or margarine
    2 medium-size onions, chopped
    1 tablespoon fresh garlic, minced
    2 tablespoons crushed dried, red chilies
    1 cup prawns, shelled and deveined, boiled, then
       cubed or chopped
    1 cup lamb or pork, cubed and sautéed
      about 2 tablespoons soy sauce
      about 2 cups cooked, drained noodles (egg
      noodles are good, but precooked Chinese
      noodles are best)
      salt to taste

Melt the butter in a frying pan, and brown the onions and garlic. Stir in the crushed chilies. Add the boiled prawns and the meat. Stir-fry for about 8 minutes or until the meat is done to your liking. Add the noodles and soy sauce, mix well, salt to taste, and serve. You may substitute white rice for the noodles, in which case the dish is called *migoreng. Serves 4.*

DHAL (LENTIL) CURRY

    2 cups uncooked dhal (lentils)
3 to 4 tablespoons vegetable oil
    ½ onion, chopped
    1 teaspoon garlic, crushed
    1 teaspoon freshly grated gingerroot
    ½ cup celery, finely chopped
   10 curry leaves
    ½ tomato, chopped
    ½ teaspoon curry powder (or ½ teaspoon each ground cumin and coriander)
    ½ teaspoon ground turmeric
      salt to taste
    4 cups water
    6 small dried red chilies (optional)

Wash the dhal, removing stones and other foreign pieces, then drain and set aside. Heat the oil in a skillet, and brown the onion, garlic, ginger and celery. Then add the curry leaves. Add the chopped tomato and the curry powder, turmeric, and dhal. Salt to taste. Add the water and cook over a low fire until the dhal is soft. If the dhal is too thick, add more water. If you would like to make this dish "hotter," you may add about half a dozen dried red chilies while frying the onions. *Serves 4. Note*: In Sri Lanka, this dish is eaten as a part of at least one meal a day. It's a good protein substitute for more expensive meat.

EGG FRIED RICE

    ¼ cup butter
    ¾ cup each cabbage, carrots, leeks, and green beans, shredded or sliced
    1 teaspoon fresh garlic, chopped
      salt to taste
    ½ cup soy sauce

3 cups cooked rice

8 eggs, scrambled and fried into an omelette, cooled, and finely sliced

Melt the butter in a frying pan. When very hot, add the vegetables, and cook for a few minutes, stirring constantly. Add the garlic, and salt to taste. Mix thoroughly. Add the soy sauce, and gently stir in the cooked rice. Add half the sliced omelette, and blend. Scrape this mixture into a serving dish and top with the rest of the sliced omelette strips. *Serves 4.*

FRIED RICE WITH PRAWNS

1 pound raw, fresh prawns in their shells

3 to 5 tablespoons vegetable oil

1 tablespoon fresh garlic, minced

½ onion, sliced

1 tablespoon crushed, dried red chilies (optional)

¾ cup each carrots, leeks, cabbage, celery, red cabbage, green beans or kale, sliced or chopped into bite-size pieces

½ cup soy sauce

1 pound cooked white rice

Boil the prawns and set aside. Heat the vegetable oil in a frying pan until very hot (but not until it smokes). Then add the prawns, garlic, sliced onion, and chilies, and sauté until the mixture is light brown. Stir in the asssorted vegetables and fry, gradually adding the soy sauce. Mix in the rice and stir well. This is a tasty side dish or entrée. You may leave out the prawns if you prefer a wholly vegetarian dish. *Serves 4.*

GHEE RICE

2½ tablespoons ghee
1 onion, sliced
4 whole cloves
6 cardamom pods, crushed
½ cinnamon stick
   salt to taste
6 garlic cloves, whole
5 pieces rampa
2 cups long-grain rice, washed and drained
3 cups hot stock or broth (beef, lamb, or chicken)

Heat the ghee in a saucepan, and sauté the sliced onion until golden brown. Add all the spices and the washed and drained rice. Stir constantly for about 5 minutes over moderate heat. Add the hot stock or broth and bring to a boil. Then reduce the heat, cover the pan, and let cook for about 15 minutes or until the rice is fully done. Add more water if necessary, because the broth may not be sufficient. Use a wooden spoon or a large fork to fluff up the rice mixture and serve. This is a very popular and appealing side dish. *Serves 4.*

HOT SEMOLINA FRY

Semolina fry is a breakfast dish in Sri Lanka, but it can be used in place of rice, string hoppers, or pittu.

3 cups semolina
2 tablespoons vegetable oil
1 heaping teaspoon mustard seeds
½ onion, chopped
1 teaspoon fresh garlic, minced
4 hot green chilies, chopped

  3 **tablespoons parsley, chopped**
  6 **curry leaves**
1½ **cups milk**
     salt to taste

Roast the semolina in a dry skillet for about 5 minutes or until light brown. Set aside. In a second skillet, heat the vegetable oil, and fry the mustard seeds, stirring constantly, until they pop. Add the onion, garlic, green chilies, curry leaves, and parsley, and brown for a few minutes. Add the roasted semolina, and continue stirring for about 3 minutes. Stir in the milk, and salt to taste. Stir and cook over medium heat until the semolina absorbs the milk and the mixture starts to become dry again (about 2 or 3 minutes). Remove from stove, and serve hot with a sambol and curry. *Serves 4.*

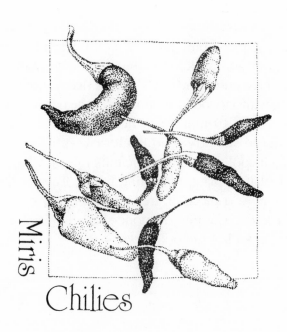

Miris Chilies

KIRI BATH (MILK RICE)

This dish is very simple—it's just a preparation of coconut milk and rice cooked together—but it means a lot to the Sinhalese people. And it's a must in Sri Lanka on New Year's Day for breakfast. It's usually served with hot sambols, but some who like it sweet have it with jaggery or treacle. The cook or the mother of the family who makes it lets the milk boil over the sides of the pan, which to the Sinhalese heralds good luck and abundance in the coming year.

> 2 **cups rice (any white rice will do)**
> 3 **cups water, at least**
> 2 **cups milk or coconut milk (equivalent to the milk of one large coconut)**
> ½ **cinnamon stick or 3 or 4 cardamom pods, crushed (optional)**
> 2 **teaspoons salt**

In a saucepan, combine the rice and water, and bring to a boil. Then cover and cook for about 15 minutes. Add the milk, cinnamon or cardamom and salt when the rice is almost cooked. Keep stirring with a wooden spoon. Cover the pan and continue cooking for about 10 minutes. When the milk is completely absorbed—there should be no liquid left—remove from the stove, and let it cool a bit. Spread the milk rice on a large lightly greased flat platter, plate, or cutting board. Then with either greased fingers or a piece of greased paper flatten it out to a two-inch thickness. Cut into diamond-shaped pieces and serve with a curry and a hot sambol. *Serves 4 to 6.*

MIXED FRIED RICE

½ cup vegetable oil
1 large onion, chopped
10 curry leaves
4 cardamom pods, crushed
4 pieces rampa (optional)
½ cinnamon stick
1 tablespoon fresh garlic, minced
1 teaspoon chili powder
2 medium-size leeks, finely chopped
2 carrots, finely chopped
¼ cup raisins
¼ cup cashews
½ cup soy sauce
3 cups cooked rice

Heat the oil in a large saucepan, and brown the onion. Add the spices and fry for 5 minutes. Then stir in the leeks, carrots, raisins, and cashews. Mix for about 5 minutes over medium heat, add the soy sauce, and stir well. Add the rice, toss gently and serve. *Serves 4.*

KAHA BATH (YELLOW RICE)

Yellow rice is rice cooked with some coconut milk and spices; turmeric lends its color to the blend. It's often served at special functions such as weddings, Christmas, and New Year's parties.

      5 cups long-grain rice
    ¼ cup ghee or butter
      2 medium onions, sliced
15 to 20 whole black peppercorns
      8 whole cardamom pods, crushed
      1 teaspoon ground turmeric powder
  6 to 8 whole cloves
     12 curry leaves
      4 teaspoons salt
      4 one-inch pieces rampa
      2 cups water
      3 cups coconut milk or light cream

Wash the rice. Heat the ghee in a large saucepan, and add the onions and brown them. Stir in the spices—peppercorns, cardamom, turmeric, cloves, curry leaves, salt, rampa—and toss

for about 5 minutes. Then add the rice, and fry everything for about 5 minutes, stirring continuously. The rice should be well-coated with the ghee mixture. Add the water and milk, and bring the rice to a boil. Then lower the heat, cover the pan, and cook for about 20 minutes. When the rice is cooked, fluff it up with a large fork. Serve yellow rice hot, usually accompanied by any meat curry, *brinjal pahi* (pickled eggplant), and a cucumber sambol. *Serves 6.*

LAMPRIES

Lampries, from the Dutch, *lomprijst*, is as rococo a bit of cuisine as you'll find in Sri Lanka or perhaps anywhere else. It is so elaborate that it requires the best part of a day to create. Although you may serve one part of the lampries "creation"— the frickadels (or *frikkadels*, a Dutch word meaning "force-meat balls") separately—the *true* lampries consists of five separate dishes—each an elaborate creation—steamed together to make a single magnificent meal.

Sri Lankans serve this festive holiday dish at Christmas, New Year's, weddings, twenty-first birthdays (the coming of age in Sri Lanka), anniversaries, or other special occasions. There are people who specialize in making this dish and whose services as caterers are in great demand for parties. But lampries can also be a party dish that is brought by guests to the host of the party.

Although lampries is traditionally made wrapped up in folded and skewered banana or plantain leaves, cooks who do not have access to banana leaves may substitute a wrapping of aluminum foil. When cooked in a banana leaf, however, the flavors permeate the rice deliciously and more efficiently.

Figure on one packet per person. It may not look like enough but the dish is quite rich and filling.

Since a great deal of effort goes into the making of lampries, you might be happy to know that it can be frozen successfully for a month or more.

Because some of the recipes involve ingredients or steps of the other recipes, be sure to read all the directions for the entire recipe before beginning.

PART 1: LAMPRIES—THE RICE ITSELF

¾	cup ghee (clarified butter)
¾	cup onions, chopped
1	four-inch piece rampa
1	four-inch piece lemongrass
1½ to 2	cups basmati rice, washed
	meat stock from the lampries curry dish (see below)
25	peppercorns
8	whole cloves
1	three-inch piece cinnamon stick
	salt to taste
½	cup to 1 cup coconut milk
½	teaspoon ground cardamom
10 to 15	plantain or banana leaves (or squares of aluminum foil, roughly 10 by 10 inches)

In a large skillet, heat the ghee, and add one-third of the onions and the rampa and lemongrass. Keep stirring until the onions are brown. Then add the rice, stirring, and cook for 3 to 4 minutes. Add the meat stock from the lampries curry dish (below) and the next five ingredients, and boil covered until the rice is half-cooked. Then add the cardamom. If the stock is insufficient, a little water may be added. Simmer covered till rice flakes and all the liquid is absorbed.

PART 2: LAMPRIES CURRY

  1 roasting chicken
  ½ pound mutton
  ½ pound beef
  ½ pound pork, with fat trimmed
  3 cups coconut milk
  1 teaspoon minced onions
  3 cloves garlic
  3 thin slices fresh gingerroot
  1 two-inch piece cinnamon stick
  ¼ teaspoon fenugreek powder
  1 two-inch piece rampa
  1 teaspoon coriander seed and 1 teaspoon white
     cumin seed, roasted and ground together
  1 six-inch piece lemongrass
 10 curry leaves
  ½ teaspoon ground cloves
     pinch of saffron
  1 tablespoon chili powder
  2 tablespoons ghee or vegetable oil
  ½ teaspoon ground cardamom
     juice of 1 lime

Cover the meat with water and simmer 15 minutes. Drain and reserve the stock. Cut the meat into very small pieces, removing and discarding the bone, skin, and gristle. Place the meat in a pan with the coconut milk, spices (except cardamom), about ½ teaspoon of the onions, and ground ingredients, retaining a bit of the onions, rampa, lemongrass, and curry leaves. Simmer 10 to 15 minutes. Add the cardamom and lime juice, and simmer another 10 minutes until the meat is cooked. In another pan, heat the ghee or oil, and fry the remaining onions, rampa, lemongrass, and curry leaves. Combine with the meat mixture, and let it simmer a few minutes.

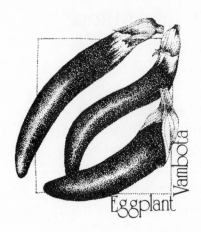

Eggplant Vambota

PART 3: FRICKADELS—SRI LANKAN STYLE CUTLETS (CROQUETTES)

1 pound beef
  pinch each ground cinnamon, cloves, and black
  pepper
  a sprinkle of salt
2 cloves fresh garlic, minced
2 thin slices fresh gingerroot, chopped
1 teaspoon ground fennel
2 cups bread crumbs, approximately
1 tablespoon onions, finely chopped
  juice of ½ lime
2 eggs, slightly beaten
  ghee (clarified butter) or vegetable oil for frying

Season the meat with black pepper, salt, cloves, cinnamon, garlic, ginger, and fennel. Mix bread crumbs and onions with lime juice and beaten egg. Combine the meat and onion mixtures, and form into small balls. Dip the balls in beaten egg, roll in more bread crumbs and fry in hot ghee or oil.

PART 4: BRINJAL PAHI (EGGPLANT FOR LAMPRIES)

    4 medium eggplants
       a sprinkle of salt
       pinch of saffron
2 to 3 tablespoons vegetable oil
    1 tablespoon coriander, ½ teaspoon ground cumin, and 1½ tablespoons white cumin seed, ground together
    ½ cup cider vinegar
    3 tablespoons tamarind paste dissolved in hot water
    1 tablespoon Maldive fish or salt cod
    1 tablespoon minced red onion
    4 cloves garlic, minced
    3 thin slices fresh gingerroot
    3 fresh green or red (hot) chilies
    1 two-inch piece cinnamon stick
    1 four-inch piece lemongrass
  10 curry leaves
    1 tablespoon ground mustard seed
    1 two-inch piece rampa
    1 tablespoon chili powder
    2 tablespoons coconut oil
    ½ cup coconut milk
    1 teaspoon sugar

Slice the eggplant lengthwise, and rub with salt and saffron. Fry in vegetable oil until light-brown. Combine the ground spices with the vinegar and tamarind paste mix. In a mixing bowl, combine the eggplant, spices, and all ingredients except coconut oil, coconut milk, and sugar. Heat the coconut oil in a skillet and, when very hot, turn in the eggplant mixture. Allow the mixture to simmer over low heat for 10 minutes. Finally, add the coconut milk and sugar.

PART 5: PRAWN BLACHANG

¼ pound dried prawns, dry-roasted and finely pounded
1 tablespoon chopped onions
2 cloves fresh garlic
1 teaspoon chili powder
2 slices fresh gingerroot
  salt to taste
  juice of 2 limes

Grind the prawns, onion, garlic, and spices together. Add salt to taste, and moisten with lime juice.

FINAL STAGE: STUFFING AND BAKING

10 to 15 plaintain or banana leaves (or oblongs or squares of aluminum foil
1 recipe Lampries—The Rice Itself
1 recipe Lampries Curry
1 recipe Frickadels
1 recipe Brinjal Pahi
1 recipe Prawn Blachang
2 tablespoons coconut milk

On each plaintain or banana leaf or section of foil, place 3 or 4 tablespoonfuls of lampries, a bit of the lampries curry, a frickadel or two, one tablespoonful brinjal pahi, a pinch of prawn blachang, and sprinkle it with the coconut milk. Fold up the leaf and skewer it with toothpicks, or fold the foil tightly into a neat oblong parcel and bake for 15 to 20 minutes in a moderate oven (350°F). *Makes approximately 10 to 15 parcels.*

CHAPTER 11

EYE-OPENING EGG DISHES

For most of my childhood, our eggs came from the chickens and turkeys we kept in our garden. Father enjoyed taking care of them, and so we always had a few. Once a week or so, we'd get a huge turkey egg. Because the chickens were free-running, the eggshells were brown and the yolk was a deep-orange. But in Sri Lanka, eggs are not eaten every morning as they are in the West. And the combination of bacon and eggs is a rare treat. Eggs appear in curried omelettes or egg curries and as a substitute for a meat dish. We'd have a few vegetable dishes and an egg curry at night and sometimes for lunch, too. And we'd also make spicy egg sandwiches for school lunch.

Around our chicken cages a passion fruit vine grew, which covered the nest boxes, and Sri Lankans say that wherever passion fruit grows there are snakes around. And that was so, and sometimes the snakes ate the chickens. But that's not surprising, because Sri Lanka has many different kinds of snakes.

My mother used to kill and dress the chickens. She also used to kill the *thala goya* (big iguana) that lived in the garden,

and we sometimes ate it in curry. Iguana tastes exactly like the most tender chicken you've ever eaten!

Although eggs were somewhat common, chicken was not an everyday treat, even for a middle-class family. Upper-class people enjoyed them often, but for middle-class families like ours, it was served only on special occasions.

And we used the eggs for medicinal properties too. If someone was feeling weak or sick, we'd take the white of the egg or the whole egg and whip it in a cup. Then we'd add a steaming-hot cup of coffee with cream and sugar. This is called an *egg flip*, and it's supposed to give you strength. Another version is beaten egg with freshly squeezed orange juice whipped with a fork.

The following recipes offer easy egg recipes with spicy Sri Lankan enhancements. Some, such as the cold, spicy finger sandwiches, are probably British in origin, but others, such as curried egg soup and egg curry, have more ancient roots.

COLD SPICY FINGER SANDWICHES

    6 eggs, hard-boiled
    1 cup grated cheddar or American cheese
    ½ onion, finely chopped
    ½ teaspoon garlic
    1 tablespoon crushed, dried red chilies or 8
        green chilies
        salt to taste
    ½ cup mayonnaise
    1 loaf of your favorite bread, thinly sliced (rye,
        herb, wheat, sourdough)
20 to 40 sun-dried tomatoes

Cool the eggs and remove the shells. Then crush the eggs in a bowl until finely crumbled. Add the next six ingredients and mix well. Cut the bread slices into triangles, or rectangular slices if you like. Spread the mixture on the bread slices. Cover with a matching slice, or serve them open-faced and topped with a garnish of sun-dried tomato. *Makes about 40 small finger sandwiches.*

CURRIED EGG OMELETTE

10 large eggs
 3 tablespoons milk
 6 green chilies, finely chopped
½ onion, finely chopped
 1 teaspoon curry powder
 1 tomato, chopped
    salt to taste

In a mixing bowl, beat the eggs well, adding the milk as you beat. Fold in the chilies, onion, curry powder, tomato, and salt to taste. Mix well. Heat a pan over medium heat and add a little oil, coating the pan well. Pour in half the egg mixture. When it is half-cooked, fold one side over the other. Continue to cook over low to medium heat until desired degree of doneness is reached. Follow the same procedure for the second omelette. Makes two large omelettes or four small ones. *Serves 4.*

CURRIED EGG SOUP

 1 cup raw dhal (lentils)
 4 cups water
 1 teaspoon butter
½ cup leeks, finely chopped
 1 teaspoon curry powder
    salt to taste
 8 eggs, beaten
½ cup spinach, chopped

In a medium-size pan, add the dhal and the water. Boil until soft, adding more water or some milk if necessary. Heat the butter in a frying pan, and sauté the chopped leeks. Then add the curry powder, and salt to taste. Add the cooked dhal, and stir well. Beat the eggs and add to the dhal mixture. Cook over medium heat until the eggs are done to your liking. Serve in bowls. Just before serving, garnish with chopped, fresh spinach. *Makes 4 portions.*

EGG CURRY

```
      8  hard-boiled eggs
 3 to 4  tablespoons vegetable oil
    ½   onion, chopped
     6  green chilies, chopped
    ½   teaspoon fresh garlic, crushed
     3  cardamom pods, crushed
     6  curry leaves
 1½   teaspoons curry powder
    ½   teaspoon ground turmeric
     2  cups coconut milk
        salt to taste
```

Cool the eggs, shell them, cut them in half lengthwise, and set aside. Heat the oil and brown the onion, green chilies, and garlic. Then add the cardamom, curry leaves, and curry powder, and roast for 2 or 3 minutes. Add the turmeric and the milk, stirring continuously. You may add a little water as needed if you like more gravy (sauce). Salt to taste. Bring the mixture to a boil. Slide the eggs into the pan, and spoon the gravy over them very carefully. Cook for 3 more minutes and serve warm. *Makes 4 servings.*

FANCY CURRIED EGG OMELETTE

  12 large eggs
   2 tablespoons milk
  ½ cup mushrooms, chopped
  ½ onion, chopped
   1 teaspoon crushed, dried red chilies
4 or 5 curry leaves
   1 tomato, chopped
  ¼ cup American or cheddar cheese, shredded or
       finely chopped
   1 teaspoon curry powder
       salt to taste
       vegetable oil or butter (about 1 teaspoon)

Beat the eggs well with the milk in a mixing bowl. Combine the remaining ingredients, except the oil or butter, in a second bowl. Salt to taste and set aside. Heat a nonstick frying pan; you may also put a little oil or butter in it. Pour in some of the beaten egg and cook over medium heat. When it is half set, pour in a bit more to coat the top and add as much of the filling as you like on one-half of the omelette (but not so much that it will be too heavy and rip the cooked-egg envelope). Continue to cook, folding the ungarnished half of the omelette over the filling, until done (about 3 to 5 minutes). *Makes 4 servings.*

HOT SCRAMBLED EGGS

  12 eggs
   2 tablespoons milk
  ½ onion, chopped (or 1 bunch small green onions,
       chopped)
  ½ teaspoon fresh garlic, crushed

1   tablespoon chili powder
½   teaspoon curry powder
½   cup American or cheddar cheese, grated
     salt to taste
2 to 3   tablespoons vegetable oil or butter, as needed
2 to 3   strips of cooked bacon, chopped (optional)

Beat the eggs well with the milk. Add the onion, spices, cheese, herbs, and bacon and beat again. Heat the oil or butter in a frying pan and pour in the egg mixture. Keep stirring until the eggs are as moist or dry as you like them. *Serves 4.*

Miris

Chilies

Sudhu lunu

Garlic

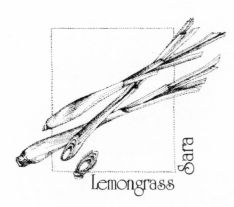

Sara

Lemongrass

Karapincha

Curry leaves

Pol

Coconut

Inguru

Ginger

CHAPTER 12

SAMBOLS
(CONDIMENTS)

Fish, beef, chicken, and seafood prepared in the Sri Lankan manner are somewhat familiar fare for Western diners. Sambols, however, are far more exotic. They have no real Western equivalents. Westerners sometimes spice their food at the table with Worcestershire sauce, horseradish sauce, catsup, and mustard. But sambols are a different kind of condiment, somewhat more like the pickle relish, pickled watermelon rind, chowchow, or other preserved vegetables that our grandmothers used to put up in jars in the pantry—and a few of us still do.

Sambols are intended to be chili-fire hot and richly aromatic to spice up a meal and provide contrast to other dishes. Some are dry and are sprinkled on; others are closer in texture to a paste. Either way, they give dimension and "kick" to rice and curry, especially if you've made your curry mild and decide after the fact that you'd like it to have a bit more character.

Seeni (sugar) sambol is one of the most traditional; it's made for festive occasions where other special foods such as yellow rice or buryani (rice cooked with beef stock) are served. It should always taste sweet and hot, and although it takes a bit longer to make than other sambols, a rich Sri Lankan meal calls for seeni sambol.

In Sri Lanka, sambols are eaten with breakfast as well as other meals. Some people like seeni sambol, for instance, with hoppers, with string hoppers, or with pittu. Lunumiris (chili sambol) and coconut sambol are also served with pittu. Breakfast pittu is sometimes served steaming hot, covered with coconut milk and spicy seeni sambol.

At most meals, just one sambol is served, although you'll occasionally see homes with two on the table.

The trick is to serve a sambol with your rice and curry dishes so those who like something hot can have it, without causing pain to the other diners. But sprinkle with caution; too much sambol can bring on full-blown running sinuses, weeping eyes, and nose blowing.

Some of the sambols take a long time to make, but at least they keep well. Eggplant sambol, for example, stores well for a week in the refrigerator, and if seeni sambol is aged for a week, it tastes even better than fresh.

You can make sambols in an electric blender or food processor, if you have one, but traditionally they are made by hand, and this works well, too.

Some of the sambols we discovered in old Sri Lankan books called for procedures that are a bit tricky in a Western kitchen such as: "Bake the tomatoes under hot ashes" or "Roast the dry fish over coals" or "Wash the shoeflowers, pick off the petals, and put them into a chatty." The following selections are not only tasty but well-adapted for Western kitchens.

BLACHANG SAMBOL

¼ pound dried prawns
⅛ pound Maldive fish or any dried fish
2 to 3 tablespoons vegetable oil
1 large onion, finely chopped
2 tablespoons fresh garlic, crushed

2 tablespoons fresh gingerroot, minced
½ cup crushed, dried red chilies
10 curry leaves
1 four-inch piece lemongrass
2 one-inch pieces rampa
1½ cups coconut milk or light cream
2 tablespoons tamarind juice
1 tablespoon white sugar
salt to taste

Roast the prawns and the Maldive fish in a dry skillet, and crush them fine with a spoon. Set aside. Heat the vegetable oil in a separate skillet, and brown the onion, garlic, ginger, red chilies, curry leaves, lemongrass, and rampa. When the onions are browned, add the fish and prawns, and continue to sauté for 5 minutes. Then add the coconut milk, and tamarind juice. As the liquid condenses, reduce the heat. Add salt to taste. Add the sugar, mix well, and serve. *Serves 4.*

BRINJAL (EGGPLANT) SAMBOL

½ pound eggplant
½ teaspoon ground turmeric
1 teaspoon salt
2 to 3 tablespoons vegetable oil, for frying
4 green chilies
½ cup chopped onions
½ teaspoon ground mustard
salt to taste
vegetable oil for frying

Wash the eggplant, and cut it into thin round slices; sprinkle each slice with turmeric and salt and rub in the spices. Sauté in the oil until brown and crisp. Chop the green chilies, and mix them with the onions and ground mustard, omitting the chili seeds if you prefer the sambol less spicy. Combine all ingredients, add additional salt to taste, and serve, preferably as a side dish with rice. *Serves 4 to 6.*

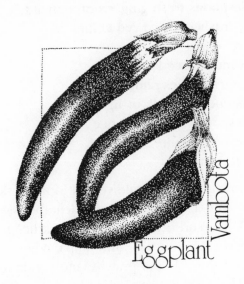

Eggplant Vambota

CARROT SAMBOL

  2 large carrots
  2 tablespoons grated coconut
 ½ tablespoon ground black pepper
  1 teaspoon lemon juice
10 green chilies
  1 teaspoon salt
  1 medium onion

Wash the carrots. Put the carrots, coconut, black pepper, lemon juice, and green chilies in a food processor, and chop them until fine. Sprinkle in the salt, add the onion, and chop again until the ingredients are well-blended. *Makes 4 to 6 portions.*

LUNUMIRIS (CHILI SAMBOL)

4 tablespoons crushed, dried red chilies
4 tablespoons chopped onion
  salt to taste

1 tablespoon Maldive fish or any dried fish
lime juice to taste (about 2 teaspoons)

Grind all ingredients together by hand or with an electric blender into a coarse or smooth paste. *Makes 6 portions.*

COCONUT SAMBOL

   1 onion, finely chopped
   2 tablespoons Maldive fish or salt cod
   ¾ cup grated unsweetened coconut (fresh coconut is best)
   1½ tablespoons lemon juice
   1 teaspoon salt
   1 tablespoon fresh garlic, minced
   8 curry leaves (optional)

Puree the onion in a food processor. Add the Maldive fish and continue mixing. Add the remaining ingredients and mix well. Salt to taste, and serve.

CUCUMBER SAMBOL

   1 large cucumber
   ½ large onion, sliced
   2 green chilies, chopped
   2 tablespoons vegetable oil
   1 tablespoon crushed Maldive fish or crushed dried shrimp powder
   2 tablespoons coconut milk
   1 teaspoon lime juice
   salt to taste

Wash and peel the cucumber and slice it. Slice the onions, and chop the green chilies. Combine the vegetables and set aside. Heat the vegetable oil in a skillet, and fry the shrimp powder or Maldive fish until golden brown. Set aside to cool. Add the coconut milk and lime juice to the vegetables that were set aside, and salt to taste. Chill before serving. *Makes 4 portions.*

DATE CHUTNEY

- 1 cup cider vinegar
- 3 cups brown sugar
- 2 cups dates (seedless)
- 2 tablespoons chili powder
- 2 tablespoons fresh garlic, chopped well
- 1 tablespoon fresh gingerroot, chopped well
- 1 teaspoon each ground cloves, cardamom, and cinnamon
- 2 teaspoons salt

Dissolve the vinegar and sugar in a saucepan over low heat. Cook until the two form a thick syrup (about 20 minutes). When the syrup starts to bubble, add the dates and spices and continue cooking over a low flame. Add the salt and stir continuously so the mixture doesn't stick to the pan. Cook slowly over low heat for an additional 20 minutes. Remove from the heat while it is still moist. Bottle and refrigerate. To make this chutney hotter, add more chili powder. *Makes about two or three 8-ounce bottles.*

FRIED ONION SAMBOL

- ½ cup vegetable oil
- 2 large onions, thinly sliced
- 3 tablespoons crushed Maldive fish, crushed dried shrimp powder, or dried shrimp pieces
- 10 to 12 dried red whole chilies, crushed, or 1½ tablespoons crushed, red chilies

   1 teaspoon salt
1½ tablespoons lime or lemon juice

Heat the oil in a frying pan, and fry the onions until they are soft. Then add the Maldive fish or the crushed dried shrimp powder or pieces, and cook for 10 more minutes. Add the rest of the ingredients, stirring continuously, and cook for an additional 10 minutes. Serve with rice and curry. Add more crushed chilies if you prefer this sambol hotter.

SENI SAMBOL (FRIED HOT ONION SAMBOL)

   ¼ cup vegetable oil
   3 tablespoons fresh garlic, minced
   3 tablespoons fresh gingerroot, minced
  10 curry leaves
   4 whole cloves
   4 cardamom pods, crushed
   1 one-inch cinnamon stick
   ¼ cup crushed, dried red chilies
   1 three-inch piece rampa (optional)
   4 large onions, peeled and chopped or sliced
   1 tablespoon sugar
   3 tablespoons lemon juice
   ½ cup Maldive fish, crushed or shredded
     salt to taste

Heat the vegetable oil in a skillet, and add the garlic, ginger, curry leaves, and other spices, and sauté until golden-brown. Then stir in the onions and remaining ingredients, and salt to taste. Keep stirring and cook over low heat until the onions are well browned—30 to 60 minutes. This sambol may be bottled and will keep for a long time (up to three weeks in the refrigerator). *Makes 6 portions.*

HEATHER'S SPECIAL MUSTARD SAUCE

2　cups brown mustard seed
3　cups cider vinegar
2　tablespoons sugar
2　tablespoons chopped fresh gingerroot
3　teaspoons salt
3　tablespoons ground black pepper

Place about 2 cups of the vinegar into an electric blender, and add the rest of the ingredients. Blend, adding the rest of the vinegar gradually. If the mix is still too thick, add up to another cup of vinegar. Once it is smoothly blended, bottle it, and it will keep in the refrigerator for a month. This mustard sauce is used in many Sri Lankan dishes, salads, meat, and fish, etc.

HOT CARROT SAMBOL

- 2 large carrots
- 8 green chilies
- 1 medium-size onion
- ¼ cup fresh garlic (about 6 or 7 large cloves)
- ½ teaspoon ground black pepper
- 2 teaspoons crushed, dried red chilies
- ¼ cup grated unsweetened coconut
- 8 curry leaves
- 1 teaspoon lemon juice
    salt to taste

Wash the carrots, and chop them in the food processor. Add the green chilies (with seeds removed, if you prefer), onion, garlic, black pepper, red chilies, grated coconut, and curry leaves. Chop all ingredients thoroughly. Add the lemon juice, salt to taste, and blend again. *Makes 8 portions.*

HOT EGG AND ONION SAMBOL

- 8 hard-boiled eggs
- 2 tablespoons crushed, dried red chilies
- 2 tablespoons finely chopped celery
- 1 large onion, chopped
- 1 tablespoon lemon juice
    salt to taste

Slice or chop the hard-boiled eggs, and set aside. Combine the remaining ingredients in a bowl and mix well, then add the eggs and toss until they are well-coated. *Makes 8 portions.*

HOT KALE SAMBOL

  1 bunch kale
  1 large onion, chopped
  2 tablespoons crushed, dried red chilies
  3 tablespoons desiccated coconut
  2 teaspoons lemon juice
     salt to taste

Wash and chop the kale well. Combine the kale and onion with the next two ingredients. Then add the lemon juice, and salt to taste. *Makes 4 to 6 portions.*

HOT PARSLEY SAMBOL

  2 bunches fresh parsley
  1 medium-size onion
  2 tablespoons crushed, dried red chilies
  2 tablespoons desiccated coconut
  1 tablespoon lemon juice
     a handful of dried shrimp
     salt to taste

Wash the parsley and drain it. Chop the parsley and onion well, and combine all ingredients in a food processor. Salt to taste. Chill before serving. *Makes 8 portions.*

LIME PICKLE SAMBOL

  2 pickled limes (see sources of specialty ingredients by mail, which starts on p. 211, if you cannot find these in your local import store)
  2 teaspoons crushed, dried red chilies
  1 medium-size onion
  2 green chilies

Chop or mince the pickled limes. Place them in a food processor, and add the red chilies, onion, and green chilies (seeds removed, if you prefer). Chop well and serve. *Makes 4 to 6 portions.*

MANGO CHUTNEY

      1 to 1½ cups cider vinegar
           4½ cups brown sugar
              1 teaspoon ground cardamom
              1 teaspoon ground cloves
              1 teaspoon ground cinnamon
              2 tablespoons chili powder
              2 tablespoons fresh gingerroot, minced
              2 tablespoons fresh garlic, chopped
              2 teaspoons salt
              2 cups fresh mango, chopped

Dissolve the vinegar and sugar over low heat. Cook until it is a thick syrup (about 20 minutes). Then add the spices and garlic and continue cooking for about 2 minutes over a low flame. Add the salt and chopped fresh mango, stirring continuously, still over low heat, so that the mixture doesn't stick to the pan. Cook for about 20 minutes. Remove from the heat while it is still moist. Cool, bottle, and refrigerate. To make this chutney hotter, add more chili powder. *Makes 6 to 8 portions.*

PARSLEY SAMBOL

      1 bunch parsley
      1 large onion
      5 green chilies
      2 tablespoons desiccated coconut
      1 tablespoon lemon (or lime) juice
        salt to taste

Wash the parsley and drain. Chop the onion, green chilies, and parsley very fine, preferably using a food processor. Add the coconut and the lemon juice, and salt to taste. Mix well. *Makes 4 to 6 portions.*

PICKLED PINEAPPLE

- ½ pineapple (fresh and a bit green)
- 1 tablespoon ground mustard (Ingelhoffer's is best)
- ½ teaspoon fresh gingerroot, chopped
- 1 teaspoon fresh garlic, minced
- ¼ cup cider vinegar
- 1 teaspoon sugar
- 2 teaspoons chili powder

Clean the pineapple and chop the fruit into cubes. Blend the mustard, ginger, and garlic into a paste, using half the cider

Papaya

vinegar. Mix the sugar and chili powder separately with the rest of the vinegar. Add the pineapple-garlic blend to the paste. Chill before serving. *Makes about 4 portions.*

RAW VEGETABLE PICKLE

    2 large carrots, chopped
    ¼ cup chopped cabbage
    ¼ cup chopped radishes, approximately
    ½ medium-size onion, chopped
    1 teaspoon fresh garlic, chopped
    1 teaspoon fresh gingerroot, chopped
    ½ cup cider vinegar
    ¼ cup ground mustard
    3 teaspoons sugar
      salt to taste

Combine the carrots, cabbage, radishes, and onion and mix together. Blend the garlic and ginger with a little of the vinegar, and mix together with the vegetables. Add the ground mustard and the sugar, and salt to taste. Make this a few hours before serving in order to allow it to pickle thoroughly. This pickle will keep in the refrigerator for up to two weeks. *Makes about 4 portions.*

RAW VEGETABLE SAMBOL

    2 cups finely chopped cabbage, carrots, and raw papaya
      (papaya is optional)
    ½ large onion, chopped
    2 tablespoons chili powder
    2 tablespoons ground mustard
    2 teaspoons salt
    2 tablespoons cider vinegar

Combine the fruit and vegetables, and mix well. In a separate bowl, combine the chili powder and ground mustard, and mix in with the vegetables. Add the salt and vinegar. Mix again, chill, and serve. *Makes 4 to 6 portions.*

SEENI SAMBOL, *Dried Style*

This Muslim-style sambol is quite spicy and takes time to make, but it's excellent and will keep a long time. And it's not as hot as it sounds either, because the onions absorb much of the chili powder.

10 **medium to large onions, coarsely sliced**
     vegetable oil for frying the onions, about 1 cup
¼ **cup fresh garlic, chopped**
¼ **cup fresh ginger, chopped**
 2 **five-inch stalks lemongrass**
25 **curry leaves**
 5 **one-inch pieces rampa**
¾ **cup crushed, dried red chilies**
 3 **cups dried shrimp**
 2 **cups crushed Maldive fish**
 8 **whole cloves**
12 **whole cardamom pods, crushed**
 4 **one-inch pieces cinnamon stick**
¼ **cup brown sugar**
 3 **large ripe tomatoes, finely chopped**
     salt to taste
 3 **tablespoons lemon juice**

Heat the oil in a deep skillet, and fry a small amount of the chopped onions at a time until they are golden-brown and crispy. Remove the onions, and drain in a colander, dripping the oil into a container beneath the colander.

In a large skillet or pot, heat about ¼ cup of the oil used to fry the onions. Add the garlic, ginger, lemongrass, curry leaves, rampa, crushed chilies, shrimp, and Maldive fish. Add the whole cloves, cardamom, and cinnamon stick. Add more oil if the mixture looks dry or begins to burn. Then stir in the brown sugar and throw in the fried onions. Add the chopped tomatoes. Add salt to taste, but keep the amount to a minimum because the dried shrimp are sometimes very salty. Blend well.

Fry about 15 minutes longer, and then add the lemon juice. Taste and add more salt if you wish. The sambol will be dry, not moist, when finished. Allow it to cool and place in airtight containers. Seeni sambol is wonderful as a sandwich spread: Try mixing it with cream cheese and spreading it on bagels or onion rolls, for example, or with sliced beef or lamb sandwiches. *Makes 20 servings.*

TOMATO-RAISIN CHUTNEY

6½ cups brown sugar
1½ cups cider vinegar
  2 tablespoons chili powder
  2 tablespoons fresh gingerroot, finely chopped
  2 tablespoons fresh garlic, minced
  2 teaspoons salt
  1 teaspoon ground cardamom or 5 cardamom pods, crushed
  1 teaspoon ground cloves or 5 whole cloves
  1 teaspoon ground cinnamon or 1 one-inch piece of cinnamon stick
 13 ripe tomatoes, sliced or chopped
  1 cup raisins

Place the sugar and vinegar in a pan and slowly bring to a boil, dissolving the sugar. Stir in the remaining ingredients, except the tomatoes and raisins, and boil for 2 minutes. Then add the tomatoes and raisins, and reduce the heat. Cook slowly over low heat for about a half hour or until the mixture thickens somewhat. *Chill and serve. Makes three 8-ounce jars.*

TOMATO AND TAMARIND CHUTNEY

- 2 cups tamarind paste
- ½ cup cider vinegar
- 2 cups ripe tomatoes, finely chopped or mashed
- ½ cup fresh gingerroot, finely chopped
- ¼ cup crushed, dried red chilies
- ½ cup raisins
- ¼ cup fresh garlic, minced
- 1 cup sugar
- ½ tablespoon salt

Place the tamarind and vinegar in a saucepan and bring to a boil. Add the tomatoes. Stir well. Add the remaining ingredients, and bring to a boil again. Then reduce the heat and simmer for about 20 minutes. Chill and serve. *Makes 12 servings.*

CHAPTER 13

YANKEE FIRE AND SPICE
Sri Lankan Adaptations of American Cuisine

Once you have mastered authentic Sri Lankan dishes and discovered the pleasure of the various combinations of flavors, you will want to carry over that excitement into everyday dishes.

Below, we proudly present Sri Lankan–American cooking —hamburgers with a tinge of hell, pasta that provokes comments, turkey legs for summer barbecuing that command notice, and hearty mulligatawny soup that renders other winter or autumn stews pallid by comparison. There's almost no everyday dish from Middle America—even macaroni and cheese— that would not benefit from a Sri Lankan attitude toward spices.

We encourage you to start here and then experiment: How about Heather's Special Mustard Sauce on a porterhouse steak? Pot roast with seeni sambol? Lamb chops with date chutney? Southern-fried chicken with a coating of garlic, ginger, onion, and flour and a side order of spiced rice? (With an odd Continental vegetable or two, we could be headed toward Sri Lankan nouvelle cuisine!)

Now, for those who wish to add the dimensions of fire and spice to everyday American cooking, the following recipes offer distinctive ways to perk up classic American meals from ordinary baked fish to sloppy Joes.

BAKED SPICY FISH

1 pound (2 cups) any firm fish (halibut, marlin, or mackerel) with skin left on
½ teaspoon salt
½ teaspoon ground black pepper
1 tablespoon fresh garlic, finely minced
1 teaspoon crushed, dried red chilies
2 tablespoons butter, approximately
2 tablespoons lime juice

Wash the fish and cut into bite-size pieces (small fish may be kept whole). Place it in a baking dish dotted with butter. Sprinkle with the salt, pepper, garlic, and crushed red chilies. Dot the fish with additional butter. Sprinkle all with lime juice. Bake at 350°F, basting continually, about 15 minutes, or until the fish is done to your liking. *Serves 4.*

DEVILED TURKEY OR CHICKEN LEGS

4 turkey drumsticks
2 tablespoons ground mustard
¼ cup chutney, either homemade or purchased (such as Major Grey's)
2 teaspoons ground white pepper
2 teaspoons cayenne
1 cup melted butter
  salt to taste (about 1 teaspoon)

Prick the drumsticks with a sharp fork or skewer so the spices can penetrate the skin. Combine the mustard, chutney, pepper, cayenne, and butter. Salt to taste, and mix with the turkey or chicken legs in a bowl. Bake for approximately 40 minutes at low heat—about 300°F. Serve hot. You may also prepare these drumsticks on an outdoor barbecue. *Serves 4.*

SRI LANKAN–ITALIAN STYLE FRIED RICE

⅜ cup olive oil
1 large onion, chopped
1 tablespoon fresh garlic, minced
1 tablespoon black pepper
½ cup (about ¼ pound) ground beef or Italian
    sausage, finely chopped
1 large green bell pepper, chopped
2 cups tomato sauce
    salt to taste
2 cups boiled rice, approximately
¾ cup grated hard cheese (such as Parmesan or
    Romano)
2 or 3 hard-boiled eggs

Heat the oil in a large frying pan, and brown the onions and garlic. Add the black pepper. Then add the ground beef or sausage, and continue to brown. Stir in green pepper and tomato sauce, and simmer for 5 minutes. Salt to taste. Fold in the cooked rice, and mix well. Cook over low flame until the rice is hot. Before serving, top with the grated cheese and minced hard-boiled eggs. *Serves 4.*

GROUND BEEF SALAD

  2 tablespoons vegetable oil
  ½ large onion, chopped
  1 heaping teaspoon fresh garlic, minced
  1 tablespoon crushed, dried red chilies
  ½ teaspoon curry powder
  3 cardamom pods, crushed
  1 pound ground beef
  1 head lettuce (any kind)
  1 medium cucumber, sliced
  2 ripe tomatoes, sliced
  1 cup cheddar or Monterey Jack cheese, finely chopped
  1 tablespoon olive oil
  1 tablespoon cider vinegar
    salt to taste

Heat the vegetable oil in a skillet, and brown the onion, garlic, red chilies, curry powder, and cardamom pods. Add the ground beef and brown it as well. Drain off the excess oil or water, and cool. Shred the lettuce, and cover the bottom of a serving bowl or platter. Add the sliced cucumber and tomatoes. Add the cooled meat-and-spice mixture. Sprinkle on the chopped cheese. Last of all, add the olive oil and the vinegar. Salt to taste, and stir lightly. Chill before serving. *Serves 4.*

HEATHER'S HAMBURGERS FROM HELL

  1 pound ground beef
  1 tablespoon curry powder
  2 tablespoons crushed, dried red chilies
  1 teaspoon fresh garlic, minced
  1 teaspoon fresh gingerroot, chopped
 10 curry leaves, finely crushed
    salt and black pepper to taste
    dash of turmeric

Combine all ingredients in a large bowl. Form into patties and fry, grill, or barbecue as you would tamer hamburgers. They are best when served with a slice of cheese and a slice or ring of raw onion. *Makes about 4* if you make quarter-pounders.

HELLACIOUSLY HOT SLOPPY JOES

2 teaspoons vegetable oil

1 medium-size onion, chopped

10 green chilies, chopped (or 1 heaping tablespoon crushed, dried red chilies)

1 teaspoon fresh garlic, finely chopped

1 teaspoon fresh gingerroot, minced

10 curry leaves

1 teaspoon curry powder (or 1 tablespoon ground cumin and 1 teaspoon ground coriander)

1 one-inch piece of cinnamon stick

2 to 3 cardamom pods, crushed

1 pound lean ground beef or lamb

1 teaspoon salt

1 six-ounce can tomato paste

2 eight-ounce cans tomato sauce

water as needed

Heat the oil in a large skillet, and brown the onion. Add the chilies, garlic, and spices, stirring constantly. Then stir in the ground beef or lamb and brown. Add salt to taste. Fry the meat for about 10 minutes. Lastly, stir in the tomato paste and tomato sauce. Simmer liquid down to desired consistency. Serve over your favorite hamburger or sloppy Joe buns. *Serves 6.*

HOT SAUSAGE FRY

3 tablespoons vegetable oil

1 pound (2 cups) spicy sausage, cut into bite-size pieces

1 large onion, sliced

1 large tomato, sliced

1 teaspoon crushed, dried red chilies

½ teaspoon garlic powder
  salt to taste
2 teaspoons lemon juice (optional)

Heat the oil in a large skillet, and brown the sausage. Add the onions and fry until golden. Stir in the sliced tomato, crushed red chilies, and garlic. Salt to taste. Cook for an additional 5 minutes. You may add the lemon juice before serving if you like. Serve hot. *Serves 4.*

MULLIGATAWNY SOUP

1 tablespoon vegetable oil
1 large onion, chopped
1 pound any kind of meat (lamb, beef, pork, chicken),
  deboned and cut into bite-size pieces
1 tablespoon whole black peppercorns
2 carrots, coarsely chopped
½ cup leeks, chopped
¼ tablespoon fresh garlic, minced
¼ teaspoon ground turmeric
1 tablespoon ground coriander
  salt to taste
8 cups water (or milk)

Heat the oil in a skillet, and sauté the onion until brown. Add the meat, and stir for about 10 minutes or until the ingredients are browned. Then stir in the peppercorns, carrots, leeks, garlic, turmeric, and coriander. Salt to taste. Add the water and simmer over low heat until the meat is cooked. You may have to add one or two cups additional water (or milk) if the mixture gets too thick. For a vegetarian version of mulligatawny, simply omit the meat. Serve hot. *Serves 8.*

POTATO SALAD WITH KICK

   2 cups (1 pound) new potatoes, boiled and peeled
  ½ cup onion, chopped
  ½ cup celery, chopped
   1 teaspoon garlic, minced
   1 teaspoon crushed, dried red chilies
   6 green chilies, chopped (optional—but this gives most
      of the kick)
   3 heaping tablespoons mayonnaise
   2 tablespoons butter
      salt to taste
   1 cup parsley, chopped

Slice the boiled and peeled potatoes into bite-size pieces, and place them in a mixing bowl. In a separate bowl, combine the onion, celery, garlic, red chilies, and (optional) green chilies with the mayonnaise and butter. Add salt to taste. (You may also stir-fry the ingredients at this stage if you like.) Combine this mixture with the potatoes, stirring to coat the potatoes well. Top with the chopped parsley. Chill before serving. *Serves 4.*

PIGS-ON-FIRE PORK CHOPS

      8 pork chops
      1 tablespoon fresh garlic, crushed
      1 tablespoon chili powder
      1 tablespoon curry powder
         salt to taste (or 1 tablespoon soy sauce)
 2 to 4 tablespoons vegetable oil (or butter)
      ½ large onion, sliced

Combine all the spices and rub the mixture into the pork chops. Puncture the pork chops well with a fork so that the flavors can permeate the meat. Heat the vegetable oil in a skillet, and cook the pork chops until well done over low heat. Finally, add the sliced onion. Salt to taste (or you may sprinkle the chops with soy sauce), and brown the onions. Serve with any rice dish. *Serves 4 to 8*, depending on size of chops.

PRAWN SALAD

 1 pound (2 cups) small fresh prawns
 ½ cup radishes, chopped
 3 hard-boiled eggs, chopped
 2 tablespoons mayonnaise
  salt and pepper to taste
 1 head lettuce, chopped or shredded
 ½ cup radishes, sliced (for garnish)
 3 hard-boiled eggs, sliced (for garnish)
2 or 3 chopped green chilies

Peel the prawns and boil them until tender and plump. Set aside to cool. In a mixing bowl, combine the prawns, chopped radishes, chopped hard-boiled eggs, and mayonnaise. Add salt and pepper to taste. Add more mayonnaise if you prefer it more moist. Arrange the chopped lettuce on a plate, and place the sliced radishes and eggs around the edge. Shape the prawn salad into a mound on the lettuce. Top with chopped green chilies. Serve chilled. *Serves 4.*

SHRIMP AND MACARONI PIE

 1 tablespoon butter
 1 pound (2 cups) small shrimp, either frozen or fresh
  a dash of salt
 1 teaspoon ground black pepper
 6 green chilies, finely chopped
 3 cups cooked macaroni
 3 ripe tomatoes, sliced
 1 cup of your favorite hard cheese, grated
 ½ cup bread crumbs

Butter a medium-size baking dish well. In a mixing bowl, combine the shrimp, salt, pepper, and green chilies. Place a layer of the shrimp mixture in the baking dish, topped by a layer of macaroni, then a layer of sliced tomatoes and a layer of grated cheese. Repeat until all ingredients are used up. Sprinkle the top with the bread crumbs and dot with additional butter. Bake for 30 minutes at 300°F. *Serves 4.*

SPAGHETTI À LA SRI LANKA

3 to 4 tablespoons olive oil
    1 heaping tablespoon fresh garlic, chopped
    1 large onion, chopped
  10 curry leaves
    2 pounds lean ground beef
    4 cardamom pods, crushed
    1 tablespoon chili powder
      salt to taste

1 eight-ounce can tomato sauce
1 six-ounce can tomato paste
1 cup grated American (or other soft) cheese
8 servings of pasta, boiled and drained (about
  1½ pounds cooked)
  grated Parmesan cheese

Heat the vegetable oil in a skillet, and brown the garlic, onion, and curry leaves. Add the beef, and brown. Then stir in the cardamom, chili powder, salt to taste, tomato sauce, and tomato paste. Last, add the American cheese. You may also add a cup of water if the sauce is too thick.

Prepare your preferred form of pasta (we recommend spaghetti, angel-hair spaghetti, or linguini). After cooking the pasta, drain and moisten with olive oil. Add the cheese over the pasta while it is still hot. Then pour the meat mixture over it. Or serve the meat sauce over the pasta and top with a sprinkle of Parmesan. *Serves approximately 8.*

SPICED RICE

2 cups long-grain wild rice mix
2 tablespoons butter
½ cup green onions, chopped
1 teaspoon fresh garlic, crushed
½ cup fresh mushrooms, sliced
1 teaspoon chili powder
½ cup coconut milk

Cook the rice mix according to the directions on the box, and set aside. Heat the butter in a frying pan, and brown the green onions with the garlic. Then stir in the mushrooms. Add the chili powder, and stir in the coconut milk. Combine with the rice over low heat. This makes a wonderfully satisfying spicy-hot side dish. *Serves 2.*

SPICY CHICKEN SALAD

    1 whole chicken, boiled and cut into bite-size
        pieces with bones removed
        a dash of salt and pepper
    1 teaspoon crushed, dried red chilies
    1 cucumber, chopped into bite-size pieces
    2 hard-boiled eggs, finely chopped
    1 head leaf lettuce, chopped or well-shredded
    2 ripe tomatoes, chopped
    2 tablespoons mayonnaise
3 to 4 tablespoons of your favorite salad dressing

In a large mixing bowl, combine the chicken, salt, pepper, and red chilies. Allow this to sit for 20 minutes. Add the cucumber, hard-boiled eggs, chopped lettuce, tomatoes, mayonnaise, and salad dressing. Stir well to coat the chicken. Chill before serving. *Serves 4.*

SPICY FISH SALAD

    1 pound (2 cups) boiled fresh fish, or 2 ten-ounce cans
        precooked salmon
  ½ teaspoon salt
  ½ teaspoon ground black pepper
    1 teaspoon crushed, dried red chilies, or 15 green
        chilies, chopped
    1 cup cucumbers, sliced
    1 cup ripe tomatoes, sliced
    1 cup lettuce, chopped
    2 tablespoons mayonnaise mixed with your favorite
        salad dressing, 1 tablespoon each
    2 tablespoons lemon juice

Crumble the fish in a mixing bowl, and season with the salt, pepper, and chilies. Arrange the cucumber and tomato slices around on the edge of a large platter and the chopped lettuce in the center. Top the lettuce with the spiced fish. Blend the mayonnaise, salad dressing, and lemon juice, and drizzle the mixture over the entire dish. Chill before serving. *Serves 4.*

SRI LANKAN PIZZA TOPPING

       dough for one 12-inch pizza
   ½ cup tomato sauce
    1 large eggplant, sliced and deep-fried
   ½ onion, chopped
    1 teaspoon fresh garlic, minced
    6 curry leaves
    2 to 4 cups grated mozzarella (or any favorite
       grated cheese) sufficient to cover the pizza to the
       depth you prefer
    6 red chilies, fried and crushed

Cover the rolled-out pizza dough with the tomato sauce, and layer the surface with the slices of eggplant. Sprinkle with the chopped onion, garlic, and curry leaves. Finally smother the pizza with the grated cheese and top with red chilies. Bake at 375°F until the crust is browned and the cheese bubbles (about 10 to 15 minutes). *Serves 2.*

UN-BORING MACARONI AND CHEESE

    2 boxes any commercial preparation of macaroni and
       cheese or four servings of homemade macaroni and
       cheese (about 4 cups)
    1 tablespoon vegetable oil
   ½ teaspoon fresh garlic, minced
   ½ onion, sliced (or ½ cup green onions, chopped)
   ½ cup fresh mushrooms, sliced
    8 curry leaves
   ½ teaspoon curry powder
   ½ teaspoon crushed, dried red chilies
       salt to taste

Prepare the macaroni and cheese and set aside. Heat the vegetable oil in a skillet, and brown the garlic and onions. Add the mushrooms, curry leaves, curry powder, and red chilies. Salt to taste. Cook for about 5 minutes, then add the macaroni and cheese. If you prefer to add meat or shrimp to this dish, add them after the onions and brown them. If you'd like to use bacon, fry it first and use less oil. *Serves 4.*

Papaya

CHAPTER 14

DESSERTS
AND SWEETS

Dessert as the Western world knows it is simply not known in Sri Lanka. What follows a meal is usually fresh fruit—whatever is in season—served *au naturel* or with a drizzle of lemon juice or a twist of black pepper (Sri Lankans even like their fruit spicy).

Although the recipes below sometimes contain ice cream —a happy adaptation to the Western palate—ice cream is very rare in Sri Lankan homes, especially in the villages outside Colombo. A woodapple cream, for example, as made in Sri Lanka, might consist of coconut milk, juice, woodapple, and treacle—never Häagen Dazs.

As far as dairy treats go, sometimes curd with treacle is served—otherwise known as "yogurt with honey"—and the curd is made with water buffalo milk. The nickname for this dessert is "the king," because no matter how full you are, your food moves over to make room for this rich, smooth treat.

The British, Dutch, and Portuguese, however, have left a tea-time tradition of *sweetmeats* such as the cakes and toffees below. You may find bread pudding, banana fritters, or pineapple upside-down cake in some homes. And vendors offer everything from iced sliced cakes to a form of cotton candy.

One fried sweetmeat that you can find made on the streets of Sri Lanka for festive occasions is *kavum*, a doughnutlike dough made of treacle and flour. It's formed by twirling a portion of dough in hot oil, but since a great deal of skill is required, only certain people in Sri Lanka can make it. These are often women who get contracts to go to a home and create the kavum on the spot for weddings or other occasions. It's not uncommon to find a kavum cook at work, turning out one or two hundred of these pointed, dome-shaped fritters for a family to give away to friends and relatives. A version of kavum is offered below in this chapter.

BANANA FRITTERS

1 **cup unsifted flour**
1 **cup milk**
  a pinch of salt
2 **eggs**
6 **ripe medium-size bananas or plantains**
  sufficient vegetable oil for deep frying

Combine the flour, milk, salt, and eggs by hand or with a hand-held electric mixer, and beat until smooth. Slice the bananas or plantains lengthwise, and chop them in two or three segments. Coat them well in the batter, and deep-fry in the hot oil until golden-brown. Drain on paper towels to remove excess oil. Serve either hot or cold topped with vanilla ice cream, drizzled with honey or treacle and/or vanilla yogurt, and topped again with whipped cream. You may substitute pineapple rings or chunks for the bananas. *Serves 4.*

SWEET FRUIT SALAD

         1 large fresh pineapple (you may use 2 eight-ounce
           cans)
         2 cups small green grapes
         1 honeydew melon
    1 or 2 mangoes
         1 ripe papaya
        ½ cup raisins
        ½ cup raw cashews
       1½ cups sweetened condensed milk
        ½ teaspoon vanilla extract
        ¼ cup lemon juice

Chop all the fruit into bite-size pieces and combine with the nuts in a large bowl. Pour in the condensed milk, and stir gently. Add the vanilla. Pour on the lemon juice and stir in well, taking care not crush or bruise the fruit. Chill and let it sit for about an hour before serving. This recipe works with almost any combination of fruit in season; you may use as few as two or three fruits. *Serves 8 to 10.*

TAPIOCA, OR SAGO, PUDDING

         2 cups tapioca or sago
         2 cups water
         1 half-inch piece cinnamon stick
        ½ cup jaggery (or brown sugar)
        ½ cup coconut milk
         2 cardamom pods, crushed (optional)
           a pinch of salt

Wash the tapioca (or sago), and soak it in enough water to cover for about 15 or 20 minutes. Then place the tapioca, water, and cinnamon in a medium-size saucepan, and bring to a boil. Continue boiling until the mixture is thick, stirring constantly

Pol
Coconut

to prevent burning. Remove the cinnamon stick, and add the jaggery, cardamom, coconut milk, and a small pinch of salt. Keep stirring until the mixture thickens again. Spoon into dessert glasses and chill. Serve cold with a big splash of heavy cream over each serving if you like. *Serves 4.*

ALUWA (TOFFEE)

COCONUT ROCK ALUWA

    1 cup milk
    4 cups sugar
    2 cups grated coconut
    ½ cup chopped raw cashews

Boil the milk and sugar together. Add the coconut and bring to a boil again over medium heat. Stir and cook until the mixture pulls away from the sides of the pan—about 15 minutes. Add the chopped cashews. The toffee should be thick by now, and so remove it from the heat. Spread it on any flat greased surface. While still hot, cut into squares and let it cool. *Makes 40 pieces.*

POTATO ALUWA

     2 cups boiled potatoes (approximately 1 lb)
  4½ cups sugar
     1 cup coconut milk
     3 cardamom pods, crushed
  ¼ to ½ cup chopped raw cashews

Mash the potatoes until they are lump-free. In a saucepan, combine sugar and coconut milk, and boil until slightly thick. Then add the mashed potatoes and crushed cardamom, stirring continuously. The sugar will start to crystallize on the sides of the pan. Add the cashews. Spread the mixtures out on a greased board or platter and cut into squares. *Makes 40 pieces.*

SEMOLINA ALUWA

  3¾ cups rulang, or semolina flour (see glossary)
     4 cups jaggery (or brown sugar)
     1 cup milk
     ½ cup raw cashews
  2 or 3 cardamom pods, crushed
     ½ inch cinnamon stick
     ½ cup pineapple, fresh or canned, finely chopped

Roast the semolina in a dry pan until very light brown, and set aside. Grate the jaggery, and combine it with the milk. Cook over medium heat until it clings to the spoon and starts to pull away from the sides of the pan. Add the crushed cashews, cardamom, cinnamon, and pineapple. Continue cooking. The mixture should pull away dramatically from the sides of the pan. While it is still hot, pour it onto a greased platter and cut into squares.

SWEET MILK ALUWA

> 2 cups milk
> 3 cups granulated sugar
> 1 cup raw cashews, chopped
> 1 teaspoon vanilla extract
> ½ cup raisins

Combine the milk and sugar in a pan over low heat, stirring continuously. When it starts to thicken, add the cashews, vanilla, and raisins. In 5 minutes, it should be quite thick. Quickly flatten it out on a greased cutting board or platter, and cut into any desired shapes. Cool and serve. *Makes 40 pieces.*

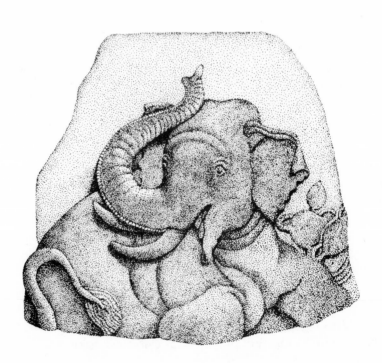

CAKES

CEYLON BUTTER CAKE

- 1 cup sugar
- ½ pound butter (2 sticks)
- 2 eggs, separated
- ½ cup flour, sifted
- 1 teaspoon baking powder
- ½ teaspoon vanilla extract

In a mixing bowl, cream the butter and sugar well—about 20 minutes. Add the egg yolks one at a time, beating continuously. In a separate mixing bowl, combine the flour and baking powder. In a deep, chilled bowl beat the egg whites until stiff, and fold them into the sugar and butter blend, alternating with the flour and baking powder mix. Stir in the vanilla extract. Pour the batter into a greased and floured baking pan (8 inch × 8 inch or 9 inch × 9 inch), and bake at 350°F for 25 to 30 minutes. You may glaze the cake if you like when it's done.

CHRISTMAS CAKE

This cake is made for weddings as well as Christmas. Some versions are topped with almond icing.

    4 cups powdered sugar
   25 egg yolks
    1 pound butter
    3 cups raw cashews
    1 cup maraschino cherries
   ½ cup mixed candied fruit peels
    4 cups sultanas (currants)
    2 cups seedless raisins
    1 eight-ounce bottle (1 cup) chowchow (a mixed
      pickle of orange peel, ginger, and other condiments)
    1 eight-ounce bottle (1 cup) ginger preserve
    1 eight-ounce bottle (1 cup) strawberry jam
    4 cups pumpkin preserves (or glazed pineapple rings)
   ½ cup brandy
   ½ cup cherry liqueur
    1 cup vanilla extract (1 eight-ounce bottle)
   ½ tablespoon almond extract
    1 teaspoon ground cardamom
    1 teaspoon ground cinnamon
    1 teaspoon ground cloves
    1 teaspoon ground nutmeg
    2 cups (1 pound) rulang, or semolina flour (if unable
      to obtain semolina, use cake flour, but the texture
      and taste will be very different)
   12 egg whites

Cream the sugar and egg yolks for 30 minutes in an electric mixer. In a very large bowl, add the butter, nuts, fruit, preserves, jam, wines, spices, and flavorings, and blend well. In a separate bowl, blend the semolina with the egg whites, and beat to a stiff froth. Fold into the first mixture and stir thoroughly. Pour into 10 to 12 greased loaf pans and bake at 190°F for 3 to 4 hours or until done. Reduce heat halfway through baking to about 150°F if the tops are getting too brown, and cover with foil. Good with any classic almond icing or served plain. This is, obviously, a very rich, aromatic holiday cake. *Makes 10 to 12 one-pound loaves.*

DATE CAKE

      1 cup white sugar
    ¾ cup butter
      4 eggs
    ½ teaspoon lime juice
  1½ cups flour
      1 teaspoon baking powder
      2 cups (about 1 pound) pitted dates, cleaned, finely chopped, and soaked overnight
    ¾ cup water
      1 teaspoon baking soda
      1 cup pumpkin preserves (you may substitute candied pineapple)
    ¼ pound raw cashews
    ¼ cup plums, pitted

Cream the sugar and butter together in a bowl. Beat each egg thoroughly, and add one at a time to the sugar and butter mixture. Transfer to a saucepan, and warm (do not boil). Add the lime juice. Then sift the flour twice with the baking powder and fold in. Add the remaining ingredients. Pour into a greased loaf pan, and bake at 300°F for about 30 minutes or until a toothpick inserted in the center comes out dry. Depending on the size of the loaf pan, *makes 4 or more servings.*

JAGGERY CAKE

　　1 cup jaggery (or brown sugar)
　　1 cup raw, unsalted cashews
　　2 cups rulang (semolina flour)
　　½ pound butter (2 sticks)
　　1 cup coconut milk
　　6 eggs
　　1 cup granulated sugar
　　¼ teaspoon ground cardamom
　　¼ teaspoon ground cinnamon
　　1 teaspoon rose water*
　　1 teaspoon vanilla extract

　　Scrape or shred the jaggery until it is very fine. Chop the cashews. Lightly roast the rulang in a skillet, combine it with the butter, and set aside. Add the scraped jaggery to the coconut milk in a bowl, and set aside. Separate the eggs, and beat the whites until very stiff. Beat the sugar and egg yolks together in a separate bowl for half an hour if you're beating by hand, or about 20 minutes by electric mixer. Add the jaggery and beat for 10 minutes. Fold in the rulang and butter. Then add the cashews, spices, and essences. Last of all, fold in the egg whites. Stir well. Pour into greased loaf pans, and bake in a moderate oven 350°F for 90 minutes. *Makes 3 to 6 loaves*, depending on pan size.

*Rose-flavored water, available in Middle Eastern and Asian food shops.

LOVE CAKE

    18 egg yolks
    10 egg whites
   8½ cups powdered sugar (not sifted)
     ½ pound (1 cup) butter or margarine
   3¾ cups rulang (semolina flour)
     3 cups (1½ pounds) raw cashews, finely chopped
     ½ cup honey
     4 cups candied fruit peel (optional)
     2 cups pumpkin preserves (or chopped, dried and
        glazed pineapple)
     ¼ cup rose water
     ¼ cup vanilla extract
     2 teaspoons almond extract
     1 teaspoon ground cardamom
     2 teaspoons ground cinnamon
        pinch of ground cloves
        dash of nutmeg

Beat the eggs (both yolks and whites) and sugar together. Combine the butter and the rulang, and add to the sugar mixture. Add the cashews, honey, candied peel, preserves, and other ingredients, and mix together. Bake in greased loaf pans in a moderate oven (350°F) until the top is brown, approximately 45 minutes. Test the cake with a knife: If the center is moist, bake a few more minutes. Before finishing, turn off the oven, and let the cake sit for another 20 minutes. *Makes up to a dozen loaves*, depending on cake pan size. (It's traditional to give love cakes as gifts.)

EVEN MORE LOVE CAKE

   3¾ cups uncooked semolina
     1 pound butter, softened
   6⅔ cups powdered sugar (not sifted)

2 cups raw cashews, chopped
20 eggs, separated
1 cup pumpkin preserves, finely chopped
1 tablespoon ground cardamom
1 tablespoon ground cinnamon
1 tablespoon ground nutmeg
2 tablespoons rose water, if available

Combine the semolina with the softened butter, and let it stand overnight. Combine the sugar, cashews, and egg yolks, and add the farina mixture, beating well. Stir in the pumpkin preserves. Beat the 20 egg whites until stiff, and add to the mixture a little at a time. Stir in the spices and rose water. Pour the batter into large rectangular (10 × 15 inches) or square (8 inches) baking pans lined with baking parchment. Fill no more than 2½ inches deep. This makes a low, rich cake, and the batter should stand no more than 1½ inches high at this point. Bake at 250°F for 2½ hours or until the top is golden-brown and the center is cooked through (test with a toothpick). Do not overcook or the cake will be too dry: Love Cake is traditionally so moist and rich that it seems not to have been baked at all.

KAVUM (PASTRY)

PANA KAVUM

Pana is the Sinhalese word for "comb"; perhaps it's a reference to the hairlike resemblance of the dough when it is squeezed out of a mold.

1 cup rice flour
2 eggs
1 cup thick coconut milk
  a dash of salt
  vegetable oil for deep frying
1 cup granulated sugar
1 cup water

Heat the oil for deep frying (375°F). Dry-roast the rice flour in a skillet, then combine it in a mixing bowl with the eggs, coconut milk, and a dash of salt. Press dough out through a cookie press or use a large frosting tip, and make any design you wish—flowers are very popular in Sri Lanka. Frying kavum is something like frying doughnuts, so use as much oil as necessary to float the dough shapes. Deep-fry the strips, shapes, or flowers until they are golden-brown. Remove them onto paper towels and cool. When cool, drizzle them with a warm sugar glaze made of 1 cup sugar and 1 cup water brought to a boil. Depending on the size of the kavum, *this may make a dozen small shapes.*

AVOCADO FLUFF

  4 avocadoes, very ripe
  ½ cup condensed milk
  2 tablespoons sugar (optional)
     a handful of raw cashews (about ¼ to ½ cup),
     chopped

Scoop out the avocadoes, and place the contents in a blender with the condensed milk and sugar. Whip well. You may add the cashews when whipping the mix or save them for the topping. Spoon into dessert glasses, chill, and serve. *Makes 6 servings.*

FRUIT SHAKE

  5 large scoops of good-quality vanilla ice cream
  ½ cup canned jack fruit, mango, or passion fruit

Combine ingredients in electric blender and beat for 2 to 5 minutes. *Serves 2.*

WATELAPPAN

Watelappan is a Muslim dessert served at many special occasions in Sri Lanka, such as weddings. It's very traditional—all the ingredients are indigenous.

½ **cup jaggery (or brown sugar)**
1 **cup coconut milk**
3 **eggs, lightly beaten**
  a pinch each ground cinnamon, cardamom, cloves, and nutmeg
¼ **cup raw cashews, finely chopped**

In a small saucepan, dissolve the jaggery in the coconut milk over low heat. When all the jaggery has dissolved, add the eggs. Fold in the spices and the raw cashews. Pour the mixture into an ovenproof bowl or pudding mold, and steam in hot water in the oven or in a double boiler until firm. Serve chilled or at room temperature. *Makes 4 portions.*

WOODAPPLE CREAM

1 cup fresh or canned woodapple pulp
1 cup coconut milk
   dash of coconut treacle or honey

Woodapple is an unusual fruit that tastes something like cantaloupe, something like nutmeg. Simply blend the ingredients together—preferably in an electric blender—chill well and serve in sherbet glasses or as a thick, maltlike dessert drink. *Serves 2.*

CHAPTER 15

BEVERAGES

Sri Lankans tend to not drink with meals, but they do drink water or tea afterward.

Some teas are flavored with fresh gingerroot and sugar or simply with cinnamon powder or cinnamon stick. But most Sri Lankans prefer the dark native tea, sometimes with sugar and milk or cream.

Dairy products themselves are not of much importance among Sri Lankans and almost no one drinks milk by itself in Sri Lanka. Instead, the teapot is always on the table in many homes, with a tea cosy over it, in the British fashion, and we drink lots of tea with condensed milk and sugar. The tea is brewed in a cloth colander (bag)—my mother always made her own colanders —then the tea leaves are wrung out tight and discarded.

A variety of flavored hot beverages can be found as well as tea: *faluda*, for example, is made with hot water and a bit of cornmeal; *coriander water* consists of coriander seeds, cinnamon stick, a bit of fresh gingerroot, and hot water. *Canjee water* is the hot water drained from cooked rice, mixed with salt and

sometimes with coconut milk or cow's milk. An old traditional drink, *barley water*, consists of barley, salt, and lemon or orange juice with sugar and hot water.

Iced coffee and beer are also very popular with the hot, spicy dishes. *Beer shandy*, which is just beer and cream soda, is very popular, especially with women.

Women in general, especially older women, do not drink alcoholic beverages. They will occasionally have a sherry. Men tend to have a drink before lunch only on weekends or before dinner on outings.

Liqueurs and hard liquor, perhaps because they are so expensive, are seldom seen in Sri Lanka. Even Sri Lankan–brewed beers such as Lion Pilsner, Royal Pilsner, and Three Coins are also considered to be expensive. And wine doesn't seem to ship or keep well in the heat. In addition, alcohol cannot be sold during the *poya*, or holiday of the full moon, each month.

In Sri Lanka, real coconut water—the whitish liquid some Westerners tap from ripe coconuts with a corkscrew—is thrown away. But flowering coconut trees are tapped by special men called *toddy tappers*, who climb along rope walkways between the tall trees and lower buckets of the sap. When fermented, this sap makes a strong palm toddy, called *arrack*, that is served straight or with soft drinks.

Although Coca Cola has established a presence on the island, a local brand of soft drink called Elephant House is found there, too. Sri Lankans generally do not drink canned soda pop. It may be a matter of taste or just as likely the expense.

Instead, they drink juice from fruits such as mango or passion fruit, or fruit syrups, either canned or fresh, combined with cracked ice and soda or with a little sugar stirred in. Grapefruit juice and fresh orange juice are common—the Sri Lankan grapefruit juice is almost lime-green in color. And limeade—lime juice with sugar—is very popular and delicious, as is lemonade.

CEYLON-STYLE BLACK TEA

The proper way to make tea is to heat water to nearly boiling, pour half a cup of the hot water in a teapot, and add the loose tea leaves (*one* teaspoon per person and *one* for the pot). Bring the rest of the water in the kettle to a full boil, and pour it into the pot. Close the lid and let it steep for 5 minutes. Rinse your teacups in hot water, and strain the tea through a tea strainer into the cups. You may add cream and sugar and lemon or condensed milk. Stir and serve.

ICED COFFEE

> 3 quarts strong coffee
> 2 cardamom pods, crushed
> 1 to 1¼ cups condensed milk
> 1 cup sugar
> 1½ tablespoons vanilla extract

Bring the coffee to a boil, and boil for a few minutes. Add the cardamom pods. Add the condensed milk and sugar, and stir well. Cool. Add the vanilla. Chill and serve over ice.

CHAPTER 16

REGULATING THE HEAT
Making Hot Foods Hotter or Putting out the Fire

You're kidding, right? You're not? You really want your food hotter? Just up the chili quotient in the dish. But remember that the complex aromas and flavors of Sri Lankan cooking are the heart of its sensuous appeal—too many chilies will drown the other interesting flavors.

Another option is to chill a few chilies in salt water and serve them alongside the meal for true fire eaters. Augmenting a medium-hot curry with a spicier sambol is another way to pack more mealtime punch.

Actually, those who are born in a culture that serves hot and spicy cuisine seem far more able to handle it than those who come to it as adults. Studies show there is no physiological difference in the palates of Sri Lankans and non–Sri Lankans. But you can acquire a tolerance of sorts for spicy dishes if you eat them regularly.

Some Sri Lankan women think that the children first become accustomed to the spicy food through their mother's breast milk. Even so, they start the babies on plain rice balls and dhal

and work up to the chili-fired food gradually as they grow up. And Sri Lankans who live in blander cuisine territory outside of Sri Lanka admit that they lose the ability to handle their spicy food without continuous practice.

Water won't cool your lips and mouth if you've eaten a Sri Lankan dish set beyond your spice threshold. Dairy products or beer are recommended, and hot tea is best, even though you'll find that it usually burns for a second before it cools you off. Other fire quenchers include tomato juice, yogurt, sour cream, and lemonade.

Irritating elements in the spices called *capsaicin*, nordihydrocapsaicin, and dihydrocapsaicin are what make the spicy hot food painful for mucous membranes in the tongue, throat, and lips. Capsaicin and its kin are not water-soluble. So you must avoid water, carbonated spring water, or soda water, which tend to distribute the fire throughout your mouth rather than cool it off.

One of the best antidotes to too much razzle-dazzle on the tongue is fat. And whole milk, yogurt, or ice cream work better than anything else to cool the mouth. A second choice is beer, since those heat-inducing chemicals also dissolve in alcohol.

Acid will also reduce the power of the oils in the chilies, and lemon juice or vinegar in small amounts may help burning lips.

Foods can be used to repair the damage as well: dhal, rice, bread, pasta, pita bread, or lentil crisps are sometimes helpful. It's a good idea for the novice to keep these items handy during a Sri Lankan meal.

Overly hot foods can hurt you now *and later*—"capsaicin burns at both ends," as one medical doctor and fan of the Sri Lanka Curry House restaurant put it. It is true, however, that stomach enzymes and juices tend to dilute a chili-rich dish, a process aided by the fact that chilies trigger production of saliva and digestive juices. And, actually, it is common black pepper, not red pepper, that is more trouble in the digestive tract.

So it's best to practice preventive medicine: Try your dishes mild, and test your tolerance before revving them up.

Chili peppers are an important staple in Sri Lankan cooking, and chilies range widely in size, color, and intensity of heat. Do not judge chili potency by size alone, since some chilies are just too mean to grow big, and as a rule, the *smaller* the pepper, the *hotter* it will be. The very hottest are said to be tiny white chilies barely half an inch long.

If you prefer your Sri Lankan dishes with less bite, remove the hottest parts of the chili—the seeds, stems, and inner membranes. But wear gloves, work under cold running water, and avoid touching your eyes or skin afterward.

The plump green bell peppers with which Americans are familiar are not prized in Sri Lankan cooking because they are too bland. But they are sometimes served stuffed, blanched and stuffed, or stuffed and deep fried. Their Sinhalese name is *malu miris*.

SOURCES OF SPICES AND SPECIALTY INGREDIENTS

If you can't locate the ingredients for Sri Lankan cuisine in your area, you can order spices, fruit, herbs, and other tropical and Sri Lankan imports from the following locations.

California

Bazaar of India
1331 University Avenue
Berkeley, California 94702

Bazaar of India
39112 State Street
Freemont, California 94538
(415) 548-4110

Berjian Grocery
4725 Santa Monica Boulevard
Los Angeles, California 90029

Bharat Bazaar
3680 El Camino Real
Santa Clara, California 95051

Curl's Fancy Grocery
Stall 430, Farmer's Market
Third and Fairfax
Los Angeles, California 90036

House of Spices
12223 East Centralia Road
Lakewood, California 90715
(213) 860-9919

India Bazaar
10641 W. Pico Boulevard
Los Angeles, California 90024

India Gifts and Food
643 Post Street
San Francisco, California 94109
(415) 771-5041

Patel Brothers
18686 S. Pioneer Boulevard
Artesia, California 90701
(213) 402-2953

Mr. Noel Perera
17336 Alfred Avenue
Cerritos, California 90701
(213) 926-8790/ 533-3315

spices, passion fruits, mangos

Colorado

American Tea, Coffee and Spice
    Co.
1511 Champa Street
Denver, Colorado 80202

Connecticut

India Health Foods
1161 State Street
Bridgeport, Connecticut 06605

District of Columbia

Spices and Foods Unlimited
2018 A Florida NW
Washington, D.C. 20009
(202) 265-1909

Florida

Patel Brothers
1930 West 60th Street
Hialeah, Florida 33012
(305) 557-5536

Georgia

Patel Brothers
2575 N. Decatur Road
Decatur, Georgia 30033
(404) 292-8235

Raj Enterprises
881 Peachtree Street
Atlanta, Georgia 30309

Hawaii

Kusuma Cooray
Cooray Products
P.O. Box 27986
Honolulu, Hawaii 96827
(808) 524-6738

*Ms. Cooray, chef at the
Willows restaurant in
Honolulu, sells her own secret
blend of Sri Lankan–style
curry powder by mail order.*

Illinois

Conte DeSavoila
555 W. Roosevelt Road
Jeffro Plaza—Store 7
Chicago, Illinois 60607
(312) 666-3471

India Groceries
5022 N. Sheridan Road
Chicago, Illinois 60640
(312) 334-3351

India Spice Co.
437 South Boulevard
Oak Park, Illinois 60302

Patel Brothers
2542 West Devon
Chicago, Illinois 60659
(312) 764-1857

Patel Brothers
2034 West Devon
Chicago, Illinois 60659
(312) 764-1853

Patel Brothers
2610 West Devon
Chicago, Illinois 60659
(312) 262-7777

Sulabha Chitnis
Suchir Enterprises
661 North Cass Avenue
Westmont, Illinois 60559
(312) 920-0115

*basmati rice, flour, dhal,
canned vegetables and fruits,
spices, teas, green chilies, long
beans, fresh produce in season*

Louisiana

Central Grocery
923 Decatur Street
New Orleans, Louisiana 70116

Maryland

Indian Sub-Continental Stores
908 Philadelphia Avenue
Silver Spring, Maryland 20910
(301) 589-8417

Indian Super Bazaar
4707 Miller Avenue
Bethesda, Maryland 20014

Patel Brothers
2080 University Boulevard E.
Langly Park, Maryland 20783
(301)422-1555

Massachusetts

Cambridge Coffee, Tea and Spice
　　House
1765 Massachusetts Avenue
Cambridge, Massachusetts 02138

Vinod Shah
3 Prescott Street
North Woburn, Massachusetts
　　01801

Michigan

Shaekar Chitnis
Detroit, Michigan
(313) 697-4044

India Foods and Boutique
37-29 Cass Avenue
Detroit, Michigan 48201
(313) 831-0056

Patel Brothers
28684 Ford Road
Garden City, Michigan
(313) 427-4445

Minnesota

Himalaya Imports
1319 S.E. Fourth St
Minneapolis, Minnesota
(612) 378-9234

Sri Lanka Curry House
2821 Hennepin Avenue
Minneapolis, Minnesota 55408
(612) 871-2400

*Heather's roasted curry
powder is available by mail.*

Virendra and Chandrika
　　Ratnayake
2022 Suburban Avenue
St. Paul, Minnesota 55119
(612) 735-7517

*herbs, spices, cordials, canned
goods—from chutney to
woodapple cream, curry mixes,
dried fish, jaggery, jams and
preserves, pickles, treacle, nuts,
rice, lentils, tea.*

Missouri

India Food Center
15-43 McCausland Avenue
St. Louis, Missouri 63117

New Jersey

Bombay Bazaar
797 Newark Avenue
Jersey City, New Jersey 07306
(201) 963-5907

House of Spices
1086 Maple Avenue
Cherry Hill, New Jersey 08002

House of Spices
9 Elm Row
New Brunswick, New Jersey
  08901

Krishna Grocery Store
103 Broadway
Passaic, New Jersey 07057
(201) 472-3025

Kumar Brothers
536 Bloomfield Av.
Hoboken, New Jersey 07030

New York

Annapurna Indian Grocery
127 East 28 Street
New York, New York 10016
(212) 889-7540

Aphrodisia Products, Inc.
282 Bleecker Street
New York, New York 10014
(212) 989-6440

Foods of India
120 Lexington Avenue
New York, New York 10016
(212) 683-4419

Morris J. Golombeck, Inc.
960 Franklin Avenue
Brooklyn, New York
(718) 284-3505

House of Spices
113-56 41 Road
Flushing, New York 11355

House of Spices
76-17 Broadway
Jackson Heights, New York 11373
(718) 476-1577

India Nepal
233 Fifth Avenue
New York, New York 10016

Indian Spice World
126 Lexington Avenue
New York, New York
(212) 686-2727

Kalapana Indian Groceries and
  Spices
42-75 Main Street
Flushing, New York 11358
(718) 961-4111

Little India Store
128 East 29th Street
New York, New York 10016

Maharaj Bazaar
665 Flatbush Avenue
Brooklyn, New York 11225
(718) 941-2666

Patel Brothers
37–54 74 Street
Jackson Heights, New York 11372
(718) 898-3445

H. Ross and Sons
1577 First Avenue
New York, New York 10028

Ohio

Patel Brothers
7617 Reading Road
Cincinnati, Ohio
(513) 821-0304

Oregon

Anzen Japanese Foods and
    Imports
736 Northeast Union Avenue
Portland, Oregon 97232
(503) 233-5111

Pennsylvania

Bombay Emporium
3343 Forbes Avenue
Pittsburgh, Pennsylvania 15213

House of Spices of New York
4101 Walnut Street
West Philadelphia, Pennsylvania
    19140
(215) 222-1111

India Bazaar
3358 Fifth Avenue
Pittsburgh, Pennsylvania 15213
(412) 682-1172

Sahadi Importing Company, Inc.
187–189 Atlantic Avenue
Brooklyn, New York 11201
(718) 624-4550

Spice and Sweet Mahal
205 Lexington Avenue
New York, New York 10016
(212) 683-0900

Oriental House of Syracuse
1706 Erie Boulevard
East Syracuse, New York 13210
(315) 555-1212

Oklahoma

Antone's
2606 Sheridan
Tulsa, Oklahoma 74129

Porter's Foods Unlimited
125 West 11 Avenue
Eugene, Oregon 97401
(503) 342-3629

India Food Mart
808 S. 47 Street
Philadelphia, Pennsylvania 19143

Indian Super Bazaar
1401 Walnut Street
Philadelphia, Pennsylvania 19104

Tennessee

Giant Foods of America
100 Oaks Shopping Center
Nashville, Tennessee 37204

Texas

Antone's Import Co.
4234 Harry Hines Boulevard
Dallas, Texas 75219

Antone's Import Co.
South Boss Road
Houston, Texas 77027

House of Spices
Cypress Plaza Shopping Center
10620 FM 1960
West Houston, Texas 77070
(713) 955-7693

House of Spices
Keystone Park Shopping Center
13777 N. Central Expressway
Dallas, Texas 75243
(214) 783-7544

Jay Store
4023 West Himier Street
Houston, Texas 77027
(713) 871-9270

Patel Brothers
6822 Harwin
Houston, Texas 77036
(713) 784-8332

Yoga and Health Center
2912 Oaklawn Avenue
Dallas, Texas 75219
(214) 528-8681

Washington

House of Rice
4122 University Way, N.E.
Seattle, Washington 98105

Specialty Spice House
Pike Place Market
Seattle, Washington 98105
(206) 622-6340

Specialty Spice House
Tacoma Mall
Tacoma, Washington 98049
(206) 474-7524

Uwawjimaya
519 Sixth Avenue S.
Seattle, Washington 98104
(206) 624-6248

Wisconsin

Indian Groceries and Spices
2527 W. National Avenue
Milwaukee, Wisconsin 53208

International House of Foods
440 W. Gorham Street
Madison, Wisconsin 53703

Canada

S. Enkin, Inc
1203 St. Lawrence
Montreal, Quebec H2X 2S6
(514) 886-3202

Kalapana Indian Groceries and
    Spices, Inc.
1763 Danforth Avenue
Toronto, Ontario M4CIJ1
(416) 698-9882

Top Banana Ltd.
1526 Merivale Road
Ottawa, Ontario
K2G 3JS Canada

England

Bombay Emporium
70 Grafton Way
London, England W1

Fortnum and Mason
181 Picadilly
London, England W1

Harrods Food Department
Knightsbridge
London, England SW1

Viniron Ltd.
Patak
119 Drummond Street
London, England NW1

Bibliography and Recommended Reading

Ceylon Daily News Cookery Book, Edited by Hilda Deutrom. Sri Lanka, Lake House Investments Limited, 1985.

Hot Stuff, A Cookbook in Praise of the Piquant, by Jessica B. Harris. New York, Atheneum, 1985.

Madhur Jaffrey's World of the East Vegetarian Cooking, by Madhur Jaffrey. New York, Alfred A. Knopf, Inc., 1982.

Sri Lanka, Singapore, APA Productions Ltd., 1985.

Sri Lanka, A Travel Survival Kit, by Tony Wheeler. Oakland, Calif., Lonely Planet Publications, March 1987.

Sri Lanka Phrasebook, by Margit Meinhold. Oakland, Calif., Lonely Planet Publications, 1987.

Southeast Asian Cookbook, by Charmaine Solomon. Australia, Chartwell Books, Inc., 1972.

The Complete Asian Cookbook, by Charmaine Solomon. New York, McGraw-Hill Book Company, 1976.

The Travelers' Guide to Asian Customs and Manners, by Kevin Chambers. New York, Simon and Schuster, 1988.

Index

About the Authors

Heather Jansz Balasuriya was born in Colombo, Sri Lanka in 1955. She is co-owner and head chef at the Sri Lanka Curry House in Minneapolis, which is perhaps the only Sri Lankan restaurant in the Americas. Jansz, her family name, is typical of Sri Lankan names of Portuguese and Dutch Burgher derivation. Balasuriya, her married name, is Sinhalese in origin. Before emigrating to the United States in 1974, she was a singer with two rock bands, the Spitfires and Savage. In addition to being head chef, Heather entertains at the Curry House, dashing out of the kitchen to take to the stage on weekend evenings. She is also a fashion designer, a model, and a mother.

Karin Winegar was born in Albert Lea, Minnesota, in 1950. She is a feature writer at the *Minneapolis Star Tribune*. She is co-author of the first professionally written dining guide about Minneapolis and St. Paul—*Let's Eat Out! The Twin Cities Restaurant Guide*. She has also authored many features and travel articles for a variety of local and national publications. She has served as restaurant critic for the *Minneapolis Star Tribune* and for *Twin Cities* magazine, and also as both restaurant and travel columnist for *Twin Cities*. Her interests include riding, sailing, travel, ethnic music, and ethnic cuisine.

Susan S. Friesen, our illustrator, was born in Niagara-on-the-Lake, Ontario, Canada in 1946. She graduated from the Ontario College of Art, Toronto, with a degree in illustration and design. Her work ranges from illustrations to figurative to large prairie landscapes. Her work is increasingly recognized in America, including recent purchases by the Minnesota Museum of Art. She lives and works in St. Paul, where she is a mother of three who loves gardening, literature, travel, and cuisine.